FR

Frantz Fanon has established a position as a leading anticolonial thinker, through key texts such as *Black Skin, White Masks* and *The Wretched of the Earth*. He has influenced the work of thinkers from Edward Said and Homi Bhabha to Paul Gilroy, but his complex work is often misinterpreted as an apology for violence.

This clear, student-friendly guidebook considers Fanon's key texts and theories, looking at:

- postcolonial theory's appropriation of psychoanalysis;
- anxieties around cultural nationalisms and the rise of native consciousness;
- postcoloniality's relationship with violence and separatism;
- new humanism and ideas of community.

Introducing the work of this controversial theorist, Pramod K. Nayar also offers alternative readings, charting Fanon's influence on postcolonial studies, literary criticism and cultural studies.

Pramod K. Nayar teaches English at the University of Hyderabad, India.

ROUTLEDGE CRITICAL THINKERS

Series Editor: Robert Eaglestone, Royal Holloway,
University of London

Routledge Critical Thinkers is a series of accessible introductions to key
figures in contemporary critical thought.

With a unique focus on historical and intellectual contexts, the
volumes in this series examine important theorists':

- significance
- motivation
- key ideas and their sources
- impact on other thinkers.

Concluding with extensively annotated guides to further reading,
Routledge Critical Thinkers are the student's passport to today's most
exciting critical thought.

Also available in the series:

For further information on this series visit: www.routledgeliterature.com/books/series

FRANTZ FANON

Pramod K. Nayar

Routledge
Taylor & Francis Group

LONDON AND NEW YORK

First edition published 2013
by Routledge
2 Park Square, Milton Park, Abingdon, OX14 4RN

Simultaneously published in the USA and Canada
by Routledge
711 Third Avenue, New York, NY 10017

Routledge is an imprint of the Taylor & Francis Group

British Library Cataloguing in Publication Data
A catalogue record for this book is available from the
British Library

Library of Congress Cataloging-in-Publication Data
Nayar, Pramod K.
Frantz Fanon / Pramod K. Nayar. -- 1st ed.
p. cm. -- (Routledge critical thinkers)
Includes index.
1. Fanon, Frantz, 1925-1961--Political and social views.
I. Title.
JC273.F36N39 2012
325'.3092--dc23
2012028786

ISBN: 978-0-415-60296-9 (hbk)
ISBN: 978-0-415-60297-6 (pbk)
ISBN: 978-0-203-07318-6 (ebk)

Typeset in Perpetua
by Taylor & Francis Books

Printed and bound in Great Britain by the MPG Books Group

CONTENTS

SERIES EDITOR'S PREFACE

The books in this series offer introductions to major critical thinkers who have influenced literary studies and the humanities. The *Routledge Critical Thinkers* series provides the books you can turn to first when a new name or concept appears in your studies.

Each book will equip you to approach a key thinker's original texts by explaining their key ideas, putting then into context and, perhaps most importantly, showing you why this thinker is considered to be significant. The emphasis is on concise, clearly written guides which do not presuppose a specialist knowledge. Although the focus is on particular figures, the series stresses that no critical thinker ever existed in a vacuum but, instead, emerged from a broader intellectual, cultural and social history. Finally, these books will act as a bridge between you and the thinkers' original texts: not replacing them but rather complementing what they wrote. In some cases, volumes consider small clusters of thinkers, working in the same area, developing similar ideas or influencing each other.

These books are necessary for a number of reasons. In his 1997 autobiography, *Not Entitled*, the literary critic Frank Kermode wrote of a time in the 1960s:

> On beautiful summer lawns, young people lay together all night, recovering from their daytime exertions and listening to a troupe of Balinese musicians.

> Under their blankets or their sleeping bags, they would chat drowsily about the
> gurus of the time … What they repeated was largely hearsay; hence my
> lunchtime suggestion, quite impromptu, for a series of short, very cheap books
> offering authoritative but intelligible introductions to such figures.

There is still a need for 'authoritative and intelligible introductions'.
But this series reflects a different world from the 1960s. New thinkers
have emerged and the reputations of others have risen and fallen, as new
research has developed. New methodologies and challenging ideas have
spread through the arts and humanities. The study of literature is no
longer – if it ever was – simply the study and evaluation of poems, novels
and plays. It is also the study of ideas, issues and difficulties which arise in
any literary text and in its interpretation. Other arts and humanities
subjects have changed in analogous ways.

With these changes, new problems have emerged. The ideas and
issues behind these radical changes in the humanities are often presented without reference to wider contexts or as theories which you
can simply 'add on' to the texts you read. Certainly, there's nothing
wrong with picking out selected ideas or using what comes to hand –
indeed, some thinkers have argued that this is, in fact, all we can do.
However, it is sometimes forgotten that each new idea comes from
the pattern and development of somebody's thought and it is important to study the range and context of their ideas. Against theories
'floating in space', the *Routledge Critical Thinkers* series places key
thinkers and their ideas firmly back in their contexts.

More than this, these books reflect the need to go back to the
thinkers' own texts and ideas. Every interpretation of an idea, even
the most seemingly innocent one, offers you its own 'spin', implicitly
or explicitly. To read only books on a thinker, rather than texts by that
thinker, is to deny yourself a chance of making up your own mind.
Sometimes what makes a significant figure's work hard to approach is
not so much its style or the content as the feeling of not knowing
where to start. The purpose of these books is to give you a 'way in' by
offering an accessible overview of these thinkers' ideas and works and
by guiding your further reading, starting with each thinker's own
texts. To use a metaphor from the philosopher Ludwig Wittgenstein
(1889–1951), these books are ladders, to be thrown away after you
have climbed to the next level. Not only, then, do they equip you to
approach new ideas, but also they empower you, by leading you back

to the theorist's own texts and encouraging you to develop your own informed opinions.

Finally, these books are necessary because, just as intellectual needs have changed, the education systems around the world – the contexts in which introductory books are usually read – have changed radically, too. What was suitable for the minority higher education systems of the 1960s is not suitable for the larger, wider, more diverse, high technology education systems of the twenty-first century. These changes call not just for new, up-to-date introductions but new methods of presentation. The presentational aspects of *Routledge Critical Thinkers* have been developed with today's students in mind.

Each book in the series has a similar structure. They begin with a section offering an overview of the life and ideas of the featured thinkers and explain why they are important. The central section of each book discusses the thinkers' key ideas, their context, evolution, and reception; with the books that deal with more than one thinker, they also explain and explore the influence of each on each. The volumes conclude with a survey of the impact of the thinker or thinkers, outlining how their ideas have been taken up and developed by others. In addition, there is a detailed final section suggesting and describing books for further reading. This is not a 'tacked-on' section but an integral part of each volume. In the first part of this section you will find brief descriptions of the thinkers' key works, then, following this, information on the most useful critical works and, in some cases, on relevant websites. This section will guide you in your reading, enabling you to follow your interests and develop your own projects. Throughout each book, references are given in what is known as the Harvard system (the author and the date of a work cited are given in the text and you can look up the full details in the bibliography at the back). This offers a lot of information in very little space. The books also explain technical terms and use boxes to describe events or ideas in more detail, away from the main emphasis of the discussion. Boxes are also used at times to highlight definitions of terms frequently used or coined by a thinker. In this way, the boxes serve as a kind of glossary, easily identified when flicking through the book.

The thinkers in the series are 'critical' for three reasons. First, they are examined in the light of subjects which involve criticism: principally literary studies or English and cultural studies, but also other disciplines which rely on the criticism of books, ideas, theories and unquestioned assumptions. Secondly, they are critical because studying their work will provide you with a 'tool kit' for your own informed critical reading and thought, which will make you critical. Third, these thinkers are critical because they are crucially important: they deal with ideas and questions which can overturn conventional understandings of the world, of texts, of everything we take for granted, leaving us with a deeper understanding of what we already knew and with new ideas.

No introduction can tell you everything. However, by offering a way into critical thinking, this series hopes to begin to engage you in an activity which is productive, constructive and potentially life-changing.

ACKNOWLEDGEMENTS

My parents, and parents-in-law, have been supportive of all my work, while remaining uncertain as to my compulsion to start a new project even before the ongoing one is done! To them I owe a considerable debt for their understanding and patience.

Nandini and Pranav ensure I do have a life outside reading and writing – and accomplish this for me with remarkable aplomb (which sometimes runs to making charts and school projects, but nonetheless!) – thank you, N–P.

Kavita for ferrying a crucial book from the US of A – thank you!

Saradindu Bhattacharya, my determined Research Assistant at the University of Hyderabad, pursued links (some missing ones) through the caverns of journal databases, and deserves high praise and gratitude for his quiet, quick efficiency in retrieving essays.

Sections of the chapter on ' A New Humanism?' were delivered as a keynote address titled, 'Postcolonialism, Suffering and Affective Cosmopolitanism', at the International Conference on Postcolonial Literatures and the Transnational, 7–9 April 2010, Chaudhary Charan Singh University, Meerut, India. Parts of it appeared as 'Frantz Fanon: Toward a Postcolonial Humanism' in the *ICFAI University Journal of Commonwealth Literature* 3 (1) (2011): 21–35. Sections of the chapters on violence will appear as an essay in the *Sambalpur Journal of English Studies*.

To Robert Eaglestone, Series Editor, Routledge Critical Thinkers, for getting me started on this book and comments on chapters, and Polly Dodson at Routledge for her several efforts, many thanks.

Finally, Anna Kurian, for comments on chapters, gentle admonitions regarding my not-infrequent slip-ups in language, and consistent encouragement.

WHY FANON?

A black man in the streets of Lyon. A white boy accompanied by his mother. The boy passes the black man and exclaims: 'Mama, see the Negro! I am frightened!' This is Frantz Fanon's famous, oft-cited, account of his 'discovery' – his term – of the nature and effect of his skin colour in *Black Skin, White Masks* (84).

Cut to an entirely different text. A black man seeking accommodation in London identifies himself merely as 'African' on the telephone when speaking with the future landlord. The description, it appears, is inadequate. 'How dark? Are you dark or very light?' The black man has to spell it out: 'West African sepia'. He then proceeds to dissect his body in terms of variations of the colour black: facially, brunette, but palm and soles of feet peroxide blonde, but his bottom, he apologetically admits, is 'raven black'. This is Wole Soyinka's brilliant satire, 'Telephone Conversation'.

What links the two instances cited here is the colour 'black' as the loci of the conversation and enunciation. Fanon wonders (and so, suggests Soyinka, does the prospective landlord) if the black man is seen as a monster: 'the handsome little boy is trembling because he thinks that the nigger is quivering with rage, the little white boy throws himself into his mother's arms: Mama, the nigger's going to eat me up' (86).

But both also document the black man's forced evaluation of his *own* body based on the white perception of it. Soyinka's symbolic dismemberment of the body into its parts, and Fanon's heightened consciousness of his skin colour, proceed from the perceptions of and demands placed on this body by the *white* population. 'Black' in both cases is more than pigmentation: it is the only identity that really matters. A *black* man. Fanon continues with his story to say how, after his 'discovery' of his blackness, he proceeds with an intense awareness of cannibalism and tom-toms, the other markers of his 'Africanness'. Black calls up and distils, Fanon suggests, entire histories of African primitivism and savagery.

The first 'story' marks a moment of initiation: of Frantz Fanon into his cultural analysis of race, racial encounters, national identity and the psychology of colonialism. The second is a literary manifestation of the same 'discovery-of-blackness' theme that Fanon documents. Black, in both Fanon and Soyinka, is more than a racial marker: it is the narrative the black man has to internalize in any encounter with the world. This encounter of blacks, browns, yellows and other coloured races with the world is the subject of an entire field of academic and cultural work today: postcolonial studies.

Postcolonial studies engages with the racial dynamics of personal/ individual and collective psychology in the colonial and postcolonial contexts, cultural practices (from literature to music), identity questions, nation- and gender-matters, economy and geopolitics. Many of post-colonialism's concerns with race, nationalism and cultural identity are prefigured in crucial and field-defining ways in the work of Martinican-born, French-educated, Algerian freedom fighter, psychiatrist and political thinker Frantz Fanon (1925–61), the subject of this book.

Postcolonialism is a theoretical approach to literary and cultural texts. It is concerned with the nature of colonial rule in Asia, Africa and South America, and native resistance to colonial domination and the postcolonial (i.e., after political independence) condition. It examines how the native was represented in colonial texts, the instruments of colonial domination (law, literature, education, religion), the forms of colonial knowledge (anthropology, census, topography), the psychological effects of colonial rule and the processes of decolonization (which means both political independence but also the process by which the formerly colonized seek freedom from colonial/European ways of thinking).

In his four major works, *The Wretched of the Earth*, *Toward the African Revolution*, *A Dying Colonialism* and *Black Skin, White Masks*, Fanon addressed several of the themes that have come to be central to all postcolonial thought. A brief catalogue of Fanon's key concerns would include:

- the conditions (political, social, economic and cultural) of colonial oppression;
- the psychology of the colonized and the colonizer;
- the processes of anti-colonial struggle;
- the complexity of the decolonization process;
- the inherent dynamics and tensions of cultural nationalism;
- the possibilities of a new humanism born out of the historical experience of colonialism, European humanism, anti-colonial struggles and postcolonial reflections on all these.

So: why Fanon? I can think of two principal reasons. One, Fanon represents the earliest of postcolonial theorists who examined the cultural consequences of colonialism and engaged with racial dynamics in the fields of psychology-psychiatry, cultural practices and national movements, and speculated about postcolonial (i.e., post-independence) societies. Second, Fanon presents – and this is something the present book argues for – a new humanism almost exclusively drawn from the experience of colonialism – and therefore is a postcolonial humanism, different from the European one.

Fanon marks an early moment of postcolonial activism, thinking and theory. His writings are always embedded in local conditions of anti-colonial struggle but with the potential to provide a humanist framework for reading other racialized, colonized situations.

Fanon was a thinker rooted in his very local ethos of the Algerian anti-colonial struggle – he was an active member of the Algerian National Liberation Front (FLN), at one time even serving as its ambassador – but whose ideas have found resonance for similar struggles by other oppressed peoples in Africa, Asia and elsewhere. Fanon's relevance has been acknowledged, implicitly or explicitly, in such diverse disciplines as anthropology, literary studies, cultural studies, feminist work, social studies of medicine and others. Fanon has been 'applied' with considerable analytical productivity and profit in film studies, media studies and literary-textual analysis.

This book calls for treating Fanon as a *postcolonial humanist*. It suggests the following.

- Despite his emphasis on violence, his work on decolonization, racial relations and the psychiatric disorders of the colonized are linked by one overriding concern: humanism.
- Despite his location in a specific historical, cultural and geographical location (Martinique first, and then Algeria under French colonial rule), his arguments are not restricted to this context alone.
- Despite his emphasis on cultural nationalism and native cultures, he eventually calls for a move beyond the native and national towards universals.

Fanon's new humanism is one that is distinctly postcolonial in the sense that it moves away from the European model (which, as we shall see, was rooted in racial attitudes) and becomes more inclusive. Fanon's reflections on the pitfalls of national consciousness mark a *self-reflexive postcolonial* who (i) understands the limits of binary thinking on race identities (black versus white) and (ii) examines critically the very national consciousness that enabled the anti-colonial struggle. Fanon's postcolonial humanism emerges from his recognition of the potential for xenophobia that exists within national consciousness, which can then become anti-humanist. The new humanism in Fanon begins when he calls the formerly colonized to dismantle not only the racial binaries of colonialism *but also* the xenophobic cultural nationalism of postcolonial nations.

So how does one begin to approach a thinker as complex as Frantz Fanon? His writings and interests span psychoanalysis, colonial discourse, socio-economic analysis, nationalism, cultural criticism, Marxist thought, psychiatric practice, philosophies of identity and African culture. He comes across in his works as a powerful, erudite but not necessarily systematic thinker – though one suspects that his dramatic (some might say melodramatic) narrative modes and his fragmented styles are deliberate strategies to prevent being classified. From his psycho-analytic *Black Skin, White Masks* to the more political *The Wretched of the Earth*, Fanon seems at once accessible and elusive. There is no *one* Fanon, and therefore, to offer a synoptic view of him must necessarily fail.

This book acknowledges Fanon's *singularity and historical specificity* (Martinique, the Algerian freedom struggle, Africanism) *and his universality*. Fanon, as this book sees and treats him, is a man of his time and place – Martinique, Algeria, France, revolution and war-time Europe. But it refuses to see him only as a product of his age, for it fervently forwards the argument – and belief – that what Fanon had adapted, assimilated and propagated was not simply ideas and concepts from his immediate setting. His critiques stemmed from a deeper engagement with more-than-Algeria, just as his insights (as subsequent work has amply demonstrated) really furthered a more inclusive humanism that sought to supplant the European one. This Fanonian version of humanism approximates to a universalism driven by a (post-colonial) concern with race relations, racial identity and exclusionary beliefs that the traditional European humanism espoused (even if in disguised forms). This is Fanon's singularity and universalism: from his immediate reading of race in French Algeria and Europe, he enables us to move to a more encompassing, indeed compassionate, humanism that works across nations and cultures.

There has been considerable debate about Fanon's appropriation as a global postcolonial theorist (Henry Louis Gates, Jr. 1991; David Macey 2000: 26–8) by ignoring his specificity as a Martinican thinker. Others note that Fanon's ideas have been absorbed by critics of varied ethnic origins and nationalities, thus demonstrating a global relevance (Rabaka 2009: 221; see also Bulhan 1985, Gordon 1995, Boehmer 2006 [1995]: 175). Fanon may not resolve the 'tension between cultural nationalism and transnationality', as Benita Parry succinctly puts it (1994: 184), but this tension between xenophobic cultural nationalism and a globalising transnationalism is what makes Fanon so productive in helping us think through the routes postcolonial nations need to take towards a new humanism.

To erase any thinker's historical specificity is to neglect her/his inspirational moments, socio-economic conditions and intellectual contexts. Fanon himself worked with many intellectual traditions: psychoanalysis, Marxism and a brand of anti-colonial thinking (from Aimé Césaire) to produce exemplary and original works. To propose that an idea forged in the crucible of a specific context cannot work when shared denominators of experience and context – such as colonialism, decolonization or postcoloniality in this case – exist across cultures and regions is to deny the power of ideas to be re-formed, adapted (not necessarily adopted *in toto*) and redrafted into the receiving contexts. Fanon's appropriation has not been uncritical – far from it in fact.

Homi Bhabha, to take just one example from many, works Fanon through the poststructuralist frame.

This does not mean, however, that Fanon in a poststructuralist frame becomes ineffectual. Indeed, many critics have been at pains to point out that intellectual movements such as poststructuralism or post-modernism do 'connect' with historical conditions (see Robert Young 1990: 119–25, on poststructuralism's links to the events of Algeria in the 1950s and the 1968 Paris student rebellions; or Robert Eaglestone's work, 2004, on postmodernism as a response to the horrors of the Holocaust). One needs, therefore, to acknowledge his simultaneous particular and universal appeal.

The remainder of this chapter locates Fanon primarily as (i) a postcolonial thinker, (ii) a theorist of subjectivity and (iii) a humanist.

FANON AS POSTCOLONIAL

Classifying Fanon as a postcolonial theorist perhaps risks marginalising his work in clinical psychology and psychiatry. However, this 'branding' of Fanon is invited by the fact that much of his work even in these domains is inextricably linked to his concerns with *race and colonialism* – a phrase that best summarizes Fanon's oeuvre and intellectual trajectory (on Fanon, psychiatry and colonialism see, among others, Vaughan 1993, Vergès 1996, Keller 2007). My reading therefore is more in tune with Ato Sekyi-Otu's (1996) and Nigel Gibson's (2003). Fanon's major insight, in my view, lies in his detailed examination of the intersection of the individual and the social, the personal with the political, where the black man's neurosis is traceable to his racialized social, economic and political conditions under colonialism. His psychoanalytic readings are almost always embedded in an analysis of the social:

- the family;
- material conditions (unemployment, poverty, violence);
- psychological factors induced by the environment (humiliation, alienation);
- the crises of the nation (the community's crisis in colonialism, the return to tribalisms, the loss of faith in folkloric beliefs).

Fanon's postcolonial thought draws attention not only to the necessity, structure and nature of decolonization (and therefore the condition of postcoloniality) but also to the dangers, contradictions and problems of the process. Fanon at no point loses sight of the fact that the processes of decolonization – such as negritude (the idea of a unified black consciousness and culture) and cultural nationalism – are necessary for the formerly colonized to really 'free' their minds. Yet he is painfully aware that these processes also have the potential to lead to some unpleasant and some downright dangerous consequences. Thus Fanon represents a *self-reflexive postcolonial thinker* who is aware of the pitfalls of postcolonialism itself – as even a cursory reading of his important essay on national consciousness shows. Anticipating the work of Benedict Anderson (as Anne McClintock points out, 1995: 365), Fanon saw the nation as a constructed and imagined entity. Exactly how the national community must be imagined – as revolutionary, enabling dissent and multiple voices, transcending the binaries instilled by colonialism – is, of course, Fanon's worry.

This concern with the ways in which a nation had to be imagined and constructed after independence was, one suspects, a domain in which Fanon was truly prophetic when he predicted that national governments in the postcolonial state would simply assume the role of oppressors, and who would 'imprison national consciousness in sterile formalism' (*Wretched*: 144). Decades later, Nigerian author Wole Soyinka (b. 1934) would echo Fanon word for word when he spoke of a 'leadership dementia' in Nigeria (1996: 153). Such a suspicion of the postcolonial nation and its leadership also marked the thought of at least two Indian thinkers in the heyday of the anti-colonial struggles: Rabindranath Tagore (poet, seer, educationist, 1861–1941, who wrote with considerable scepticism about nationalism) and Mahatma Gandhi (1869–1948, who argued that the Congress Party, which was at the forefront of the anti-colonial struggle, must disband after independence was achieved and its members made to serve the country in other capacities). We see Fanon's worries over the postcolonial state manifest also in writers like Ghanian Aye Kwei Armah (b. 1939), whose novel *The Beautyful Ones are Not Yet Born* (1988) wondered 'how could such a thing turn so completely into this other thing?' (85), about the promise and potential of the anticolonial struggle that had morphed into the hideous monster of the postcolonial state. Similar sentiments are seen in Indian-born Salman Rushdie (b. 1947) and Indian-born Canadian writer Rohinton Mistry (b. 1952), George Lamming (b. 1927) from the Caribbean and Isabelle Allende (b. 1942) from Chile, whose writings constitute what I have elsewhere termed the post-colonial novel of disillusionment (2010: 82).

Fanon was alert to the dualisms on which all colonialism was based: the dualisms of rational, good, pure white versus irrational, evil, impure black (what is now referred to as 'manicheanism'). But Fanon was also alert to the potential of a decolonising nation to slip into the *legacy* of this dualism. Thus, Fanon was the first postcolonial theorist to warn us that after political independence, 'some blacks can be whiter than the whites' (*Wretched*: 93). As we note on an everyday basis – if I might shift focus away from the literary-imaginative to the material – the new elites in decolonized nations become the new colonizers in numerous 'Third World' nations. The easy division of the 'good people' (colonized) on one side and the 'bad people' (colonizers) on the other that prevailed during the colonial era does not exist any more in this state of (alleged) decolonization. It is precisely because of an inverted but still existing colonial legacy of dualism that the post-colonial nation requires a whole new humanism, one that Fanon hoped for. When *Black Skin White Masks* ends, the cautious Fanon, imbued with prophetic forebodings about the nature of the postcolonial nation state, calls for a move beyond the antagonistic dualism of racial identity (black versus white), and towards a mature treatment of the Other (Alessandrini 2010: 11). This is the new humanism, where the racial binaries that drove imperialism, and even (especially?) its civilizing mission (which argued that the superior white race must civilize the inferior black or brown one), are abandoned.

FANON AS A THEORIST OF SUBJECTIVITY

Fanon might be profitably read as one of the first postcolonial theorists who explored the nature of the colonized's subjectivity and subject-formation in the colonial situation. He was one of the first to ponder over the processes through which the colonized fashioned himself (Fanon's gendered analysis is to be emphasized) a new subjectivity.

Fanon begins by suggesting that in the violent, racist colonial situation the colonized had had his personality, psyche and consciousness destroyed. The colonized, writes Fanon, is 'battered' by primitivism, the absence of any real intellectual activity and consciousness in general (*Black Skin*: 84–5). Fanon suggests a breakdown of self-consciousness, a sense of the self and of identity, in the colonial situation. So how does the colonized black man emerge from this condition of total self-annihilation? There is, in Fanonian thought, considerable emphasis on self-fashioning.

Lacking identity, the colonized seeks recognition, identification as white *by* the white. The colonised denied identity is now concerned less with identity than with *identification*, and the position from which identification proceeds – that of the white man and white culture (Bhabha 2009a: 63–4). That is, the black man lacking all sense of self, seeks an identity which only the white man, and *his* white culture, can bestow. The black man whose own culture and consciousness have been destroyed seeks refuge by looking for acknowledgement of some kind from and within the alien, white culture. He fashions himself after the white master, by putting on an ill-fitting 'white mask', or more accurately a set of masks, all roles the white man wishes the black man to play. There is, therefore, a constant slippery shift between black and white for the colonized. The whole problem of identity, as Fanon sees it, is the lack of a clear identity for the colonized, as we shall see in Chapter 3.

Fanon also proposes violence as a mode of self-realization and self-fashioning: 'The colonized subject discovers reality and transforms it through his praxis, his deployment of violence and his agenda for liberation' (*Wretched*: 21). Violence is a means of survival and a mode of creating agency (the ability to determine the course of one's life and actions) when, in the colonial context, there is little choice or power to the colonized. (Later postcolonial theorists have noted the centrality of the anti-colonial struggle, whether violent or non-violent, as a mode of achieving a sense of self among the natives/colonized: see Leela Gandhi 1999: 112; Bhabha 2004: xxxvl; Srivastava 2010.)

It is this *refashioned, formerly colonized subject that marks the rise of a new humanism in Fanon*. Without the process of decolonization that enables the rise of a new consciousness that rejects European racial-ized humanism and the anti-colonial's xenophobia, there can be no truly inclusive humanism. In other words: a new humanism emerges only from the once-colonized (non-white) native who has, through violence, decolonization and self-fashioning, recreated himself as a free individual who refuses both cultural nationalism's xenophobia as well as European humanism.

FANON AS A HUMANIST

This book treats Fanon as imagining – an imagining not proved right historically when we look at the civil unrest and ethnicide in Algeria, and more recently in Tunisia – a *new humanism*. Despite the emphasis on violence, this book suggests in its last chapter that Fanon's work offers us a humanist framework that firstly, moves beyond the violence and historical specificities of anti-colonial struggles and Africa; secondly, avoids the racial, colonial and capitalist problems of traditional European Enlightenment humanisms; and finally, reflects on the potential for anti-humanist xenophobia and a frightening return to racial and ethnic binaries within postcolonial cultural nationalisms.

Fanon's humanism, this book suggests, is arrived at through a specific trajectory, which may be summarized in four key steps.

1 Fanon explores the colonial conditions where racism and oppression annihilate the native's sense of self, his cultural identity and his consciousness. Fanon argues a case for colonialism as anti-humanist in this sense, even though much of colonialism's civilizing mission (the colonial project of 'uplifting' the so-called savage native in Africa and Asia through European education, Christianity and law) was ostensibly driven by a humanist vision of the unity and inherent equality of all mankind. Here Fanon speaks of the psychiatric disorders, violence and discontent that mark the colonized.

2 Fanon traces the colonized's return to a sense of self. Initially, the black man puts on 'white masks', hoping to be acknowledged by the white man. Realizing that he will never be fully white, the colonized man now constantly slips between identities of black and white.

3 As a result of this confused, split psyche, the colonized discovers an urgent need to anchor himself in forms of action that can help him attain a sense of the self. Fanon sees violence as a means through which the colonized not only fights the colonial master but seeks an affirmation of himself. In other words, violence becomes a means of discovering a sense of the self.

4 In the period of decolonization, it is the cultural nationalism of anti-colonial struggles that helps the colonized develop a sense of the self. It embeds the formerly colonized back into his culture. But, Fanon warns, there is the risk that cultural nationalism can operate along the same lines as colonialism: by excluding some ethnic

groups, identities and peoples. The colonized who stops to reflect on his own process of self-fashioning, who has discovered the essential anti-humanism of European thought, would be on the alert that postcolonial nations should not lapse into xenophobia. Fanon argues that the truly liberated postcolonial would take the humanism of Europe but without its racial aspects. He would take the self-fashioning of the postcolonial situation but without its xenophobia. That is, what Fanon is proposing is that the self-fashioned post-colonial is self-reflexive about his own conditions, learns to distrust cultural nationalism and favours a universal humanism that is really 'to understand and to love' (*Black Skin*: 1). A new humanism can emerge only from the formerly colonized who is self-aware, who has a 'concept of the future of mankind' (*Wretched:* 143) that draws on the experience of the anti-colonial struggle, that seeks inspiration from Europe's history of humanism but abandons both European exclusionary humanism and postcolonial xenophobic nationalisms.

This book follows this four-part route to reading Fanon. After a brief account of his life and his intellectual influences, I move on to discuss Fanon's analysis of the racial conditions of colonialism (Chapters 3 and 4). Here I explore Fanon's explication of the processes of self-annihilation in colonialism, which corresponds to points 1 and 2 in Fanonian thought listed above. The next chapters, 5 and 6, on violence, examine Fanon's writings on violence where he treats violence as a step towards the rediscovery *and* reconstruction of the self of the colonized. This corresponds to point 3 above. Chapters 7 and 8 deal with Fanon's studies and critiques of decolonization, and correspond to point 4 above. Finally, Chapter 9 excavates the humanism within Fanon's thought, focusing on his ethics of recognition, collective ethics and universalism.

KEY IDEAS

1

FANON

Life in a Revolution

Frantz Fanon's writing is inextricably linked to his political activism in the Algerian freedom struggle. What we now have as Fanon's oeuvre consists, in the main, of lectures, journalism and essays he had published in psychiatric journals and radical periodicals or delivered at various political and literary forums. His writing embodies, literally, his life *in* a revolution.

Frantz Fanon was born in Martinique, on 20 July 1925, the fifth of eight children, and grew up in Fort-de-France. Martinique is a tiny island, about 1,000 square kilometers in area, one of a group of Caribbean islands. It was colonized in the seventeenth century and was, when Fanon was born, an 'overseas department' of France. It had been central to the slave economy and trade – a fact of history of which Fanon was very conscious. As he would put it in *Black Skin, White Masks*: 'I am not a slave of the Slavery that dehumanized my ancestors' (179).

Fanon's great-grandfather had been the son of a slave, but had acquired land and taken to farming cocoa. Fanon's father, Félix Casimir, worked for the government in the customs department, and his mother, Eléonore, ran a store. The family was fairly well off with the double income (they even had a second house), but there were several signs of extreme poverty around them. Fanon attended the *lycée*, and it was at the local library that Fanon may have acquired his wide-ranging education through his voracious reading, especially in philosophy and literature. Classical reading was, of course, easily available, and Fanon seems to have used his time very well.

At school, Creole (a mix of French and African languages) was strictly prohibited, and French alone was acceptable. This linguistic hierarchy might have given the young Fanon an insight into the colonial condition (even though he probably had almost no contact with the Europeans in Martinique). Years later, perhaps recalling this injunction from his school days, Fanon would underscore the centrality of language to colonialism: the first chapter of *Black Skin* is on 'the negro and language'.

It was at the *lycée* that Fanon first encountered the figure who would influence his thought the most at this stage – the African-Martinican poet, writer and politician Aimé Césaire (1913–2008), who had joined the school as a teacher. Césaire, as Fanon would admit, instilled in him and his schoolmates, and perhaps an entire generation, the pride of being black. In 1939 Césaire would publish his *Notebook of a Return to My Native Land*. Fanon would be deeply influenced by the work, and it is said he could recite long passages from it.

In 1940 France had signed an armistice with the German army, but this was rejected by General Charles de Gaulle. Martinique's governors and mayors pledged their support for the Allies in the war, and offered its services. A few months later the region's port and harbour were locked down under US supervision as part of the war effort. A large number of sailors were therefore deputed to stay on the site – and this would have given the Martinican boys a sight of white military power as never before.

In 1943, at the age of seventeen, Fanon ran away to Dominica to join the French army, but was rejected because of his age and sent back home. His first attempt to be part of the colonial/white set-up had just failed. In the years preceding his attempted military career, the events unfolding around him would have given him more insights into the racial conditions of the region. There had been some unrest in Martinique in this period. In 1942 some of the natives refused to sing the French national anthem, and fights between white sailors and native boys were common.

In July 1944 a decision was taken to send volunteers to fight for the French army. Fanon again volunteered and on 12 March 1944 sailed to Casablanca and was later deputed to Oran. It would be a historic journey, for at the end of it Fanon would understand more about race and colonialism than he had ever had from all his reading and more or less provincial life.

In Algeria Fanon witnessed for the first time colonialism-induced starvation among the Arab natives. The white soldiers and administrators led comfortable lives, while the rest of Morocco languished in poverty and discontent. Christians, Fanon would have seen, lived in fairly pleasant houses while Muslims struggled to feed their families. Soldiers from the Caribbean and Africa were treated (and even dressed) differently. The black soldiers were treated as superior to the Arab ones (Macey 2000: 93). This might have been the moment of Fanon's discovery of the cultural politics of colonialism as well, when he saw how particular cultures were tolerated and even protected at the cost of others.

He was later sent on missions to the Rhone Valley. It was winter and Fanon, along with his Senegalese comrades, suffered in the bitter cold. On the front, watching the Senegalese soldiers being sent in first to face enemy fire, while the French merely followed, Fanon discovered the extent of both racism and colonialism. On one such excursion, Fanon was hit by shrapnel and suffered a serious chest injury. For his bravery and injuries he was decorated with the *Croix de Guerre*, but his army career was definitely over. Fanon had seen what it was to be black in a white army defending a European power and fighting for 'an obsolete ideal', as he wrote in a letter from the front (Macey 2000: 103). The war was, literally, an eye-opener for Fanon.

In October of 1945 Fanon headed back to Martinique, and rejoined the *lycée* to complete his education. It was also in 1945 that Césaire ran for parliament, and Fanon was one of the many who joined forces to help Césaire win his campaign for the post of Mayor of Fort-de-France.

Meanwhile, after the army stint, Fanon was looking at various trajectories for higher studies. He left for Lyon where he first considered the law, but in a complete shift of interest (he spent three weeks studying law!) he turned to dentistry at the University of Lyon. It was in Lyon that Fanon experienced the event from which he would draw his extraordinary observations about racism.

One day in Lyon, Fanon would hear a child cry out, 'Look, a negro ... Mum, look a negro. I'm frightened! Frightened! Frightened!' It was a defining moment in the making of the postcolonial thinker for he 'discovers' his blackness in this incident (*Black Skin*: 84).

At Lyon Fanon met other Africans. He also noted, after a few months of stay, that the Algerians in the city were often tagged as criminals – many driven to crime due to their poverty. Fanon was yet again experiencing the enormous gap between races, this time in a European setting.

At the University of Lyon Fanon studied medicine but then turned towards psychiatry. It is believed that he may have been an occasional visitor or even a member of the student body of the Communist Party of France during this period, but no proof of this is available (Macey 2000: 124).

Not a very social person, Fanon spent a lot of time reading. Fanon's extensive and voracious reading in philosophy continued – especially new journals like *Esprit*, and Jean-Paul Sartre's *Présence Africaine*, but also the African American novelist and essayist, Richard Wright (1908–60), the African American writer of crime fiction (who published much of his early work during his imprisonment for violent crime), and Chester Himes (1909–84) – and he also spent time editing his own magazine, *Tam-tam* (Macey 2000: 129). Fanon was also reading widely in contemporary psychoanalysis, especially the French Jacques Lacan (1901–81) and Germaine Guex (1904–84), a Swiss psychoanalyst. At the medical school, Fanon was also conducting personal observations and free association tests. He was keen to see what related terms the word 'negro' would conjure up among whites. Fanon discovered that of his four hundred participants, nearly all of them used terms from already existing stereotypes about the blacks: sports, penis, boxer, savage, sin, sex, etc. He would also encounter, even among the educated students of the university, absurd prejudices about blacks. Many continued to believe, for instance, myths about black cannibalism and the absence of black culture. That racism revolves around essentialisms now became clear to the young Fanon.

Lyon provided his personal life with its own intrigues and adventures. In what many surely, at the time, viewed as a misalliance, Fanon got involved with a fellow medical student, the French Michelle, with whom he had a daughter. Fanon initially refused to acknowledge the child as his own. It was years later, and after considerable persuasion from his family and friends, that he did, but this daughter, Mirielle, never met her father. Fanon then became involved with Marie-Josephe Dublé (Josie). Josie would become his amanuensis, and the work she transcribed as Fanon dictated his thoughts would become *Black Skin, White Masks*.

Fanon's clinical training came to an end in 1951 and he took up a temporary post at a hospital in Dôle. At the hospital, Fanon made his first case records of patients with psychotic disorders – cases that would eventually help him formulate theories of colonial psychoanalytic practice.

Fanon was hoping to submit his dissertation to qualify as a doctor of medicine, but his superiors rejected the idea, saying it was too subjective and experimental. This manuscript, which contained Fanon's first engagement, though brief, with Jacques Lacan, would appear as *Black Skin*. The first essay from this work appeared in the May 1951 issue of *Esprit* and Editions de Seuil would go on to publish the complete book in 1952. Fanon then took up a more conventional medical topic (Friedrich's disease), worked through it in more acceptable (to the academic system) ways and successfully defended it on 29 November 1951.

Black Skin appeared in print in 1952, and puzzled readers with its mix of literary, psychoanalytic and philosophic observations. Fanon had broken conventions in mixing genres and disciplines here. The year was also significant for another reason. Dr Frantz Fanon and Josie got married in 1952 and Fanon took up a position at the Saint-Alban hospital. Here the doctors, led by François Tosquelles, conducted experiments in psychotherapy, focusing (unusually for the prevalent medical climate of the time) on the social contexts of mental illness. The same year Fanon visited Martinique, perhaps with the idea of setting up psychiatric practice there. Quickly realizing that there were no prospects in his homeland, Fanon returned to Saint-Alban. He would not see Martinique again.

In June 1953 Fanon entered a competitive exam for a medical position, and having passed it, qualified as a psychiatrist. Armed with this Fanon was relatively freer to look for other jobs. In November 1953 he was appointed by the government as a psychiatrist at the Blida-Joinville hospital, Algeria's largest psychiatric facility. Fanon now began living with his wife in a quarter on the campus itself, where their only son, Olivier, would be born in 1955. Alongside his practice Fanon began publishing scholarly essays in psychiatric journals (Macey's biography offers a detailed bibliography; also see Butts 1979, Bulhan 1985, Lebeau 1998, Macey 1999). His hospital life was extremely busy – indeed one of the things that strike us is the amount of energy Fanon seemed to have had.

Around the year he joined Blida, Algeria was beginning to show distinct signs of unrest and tensions against the French 'occupation'. Fanon now saw how the town was racially segregated between the dirty and poor native segment and the clean and orderly French one – something he would draw attention to in *Wretched*. In November 1954 violence erupted, French soldiers were killed and explosions rocked Algiers. Guerrillas who had massed in the various regions began attacks on government sites. The Algerian insurgency had begun – it was to become one of the longest and bloodiest wars of the continent. The French army was brutal in its counter-insurgency measures – with disappearances, executions and torture. The Front de Libération Nationale (FLN), the organization for the Algerian freedom struggle, was formed in late 1954/early 1955 and actively took similar brutal executions to their French colonizers, targeting French civilians and families which, in turn, attracted worse reprisals by French troops.

Continuing his interest in the operations of colonial medicine, especially psychiatry, that he had begun at Dôle, Fanon now found the psychiatric practice at Blida problematic. Fanon was unable to come to terms with the role he played in the colonial medical structure that was the hospital. He realized that hospitals such as Blida were not keen on treating the natives. The psychiatric theories followed by doctors and nurses simply assumed the innate savagery, criminality and propensity to violence of the Arab and the black man. Fanon realized in his studies of black patients, that their supposed pathological problems were mainly psychosomatic, the result of mental disturbances induced by the social contexts of racism and colonialism. Policemen (European) came to him for help in strengthening themselves to torture FLN guerrillas without become violent towards their families. Algerian combatants and civilians sought help, having suffered physiological and psychological disturbances after prolonged exposure to violence. Treating French policemen and Arab patients, Fanon realized that colonialism engendered violence in *both* victim and perpetrator.

Fanon made careful notes on these cases. His essay 'Colonial War and Mental Disorders' in *Wretched* (an early version of this essay appeared in a journal, *Consciences Algériennes* in 1955) and the key, and controversial, thesis on violence in *Wretched* drew upon these clinical experiences. He would argue that the very social conditions of colonialism engendered violence – violence was not immanent to the blacks, it was produced in them by the injustice of colonial domination. Fanon also noted that the colonial structure that facilitated and *sanctioned* torture and violence on the part of the ruling class, induced psychological disorders among the perpetrators of that violence.

Further insights into colonial medicine and psychiatry came from his reading of psychoanalytic works such as O. Mannoni's *Prospero and Caliban: The Psychology of Colonization* (1950, English trans. 1964). Mannoni argued that all colonization is based on a relationship between psychological types: the authoritative white man and the dependent black one. Fanon began to see how European models of psychoanalysis located all psychotic conditions in individual psyches while ignoring very real material conditions – such as racism or colonialism. Fanon himself would observe that it was the lived experience of the blacks that induced psychotic behavior.

By now Fanon's ideological position on psychiatry was clearly at odds with prevalent opinions. With racialized inequality, poverty and large-scale unemployment all around him, Fanon was beginning to see colonialism's horrific effects with greater clarity. Around this time he also established contact with the FLN, and the anti-colonial Algerian war quickly gained his sympathies. He may even have considered joining the guerrillas and the FLN forces, but discovered that, as a psychiatrist he could contribute to the FLN cause in other ways. Thus, his medical practice, intensive reading and political work all began to come together, as his analysis of the colonial condition began to deepen.

As a doctor, Fanon might have also tried some experimental methods in psychiatry, including music therapy, new forms of Thematic Apperception Tests, and studies he conducted with, and wrote about, with younger colleagues like Charles Geronimi and François Sanchez. However, circulating accounts of his radicalism in treatment procedures might be, as commentators have pointed out, simply exaggerated (Vergès 1996).

In 1956 Fanon travelled to Paris to participate in a massive international congress organized by *Présence Africaine* (Richard Wright was at the Congress, as was the Senegalese writer and activist Alioune Diop, 1910–80) where he read a paper on 'Racism and Culture' (reprinted in *Toward the African Revolution*).

His discomfort with his job, and the entire medical practice, was mounting. Now certain that psychiatry practised under the aegis of a colonial regime was not his domain, Fanon finally resigned from his post in 1956. In his letter to the Minister he stated that the Arab was 'systematically' dehumanized in the colonial set-up, and colonial psychiatry did not solve his, the Arab's, problems. Fanon wrote:

> If psychiatry is the medical technique that aims to enable man no longer to be stranger to his environment, I owe it to myself to affirm that the Arab, permanently an alien in his own country, lives in a state of absolute depersonalization.
>
> ('Letter to the Resident Minister', *African:* 53)

He went on to state in no uncertain terms:

> the social structure existing in Algeria was hostile to any attempt to put the individual back where he belonged
>
> (*African*: 53).

In January 1957 the French government expelled Fanon from Algeria. He became more active in the FLN, especially after his expulsion and arrival in Tunis (even though the internal politics of the organization were not exactly clear to him initially). He worked as editor for the French Algerian newspaper *El Moudjahid*, participated in political discussions, and may have addressed student groups at the University of Tunis. His writings during this time reveal an extreme disillusionment with the French left. His 'French Intellectuals and Democrats and the Algerian Revolution' opened with the powerful statement 'one of the first duties of intellectuals and democratic elements in colonialist countries is unreservedly to support the national aspirations of colonized peoples' (*African*: 76). He went on to attack the French left for being in a 'paradoxical and increasingly sterile situation' (89), and called upon it to support the Algerian cause uninhibitedly, to become 'concretely involved' in the struggle (90).

Fanon was attached to the Manouba clinic in Tunis (he worked under the name of 'Dr Fares' here) where he attempted certain reforms in treatment procedures. In addition to his responsibilities here, the indefatigable Fanon was also working at the Charles-Nicolle general hospital, working to set up a psychiatric day clinic there. He was also treating nurses from the health service. He met victims of torture who could not even turn on an electric switch because memories of electric shocks at the hands of the military would traumatize them. He met victims of depression, hallucinations and unexplained violence – all of which he traced back to the tortures. News of tortures, midnight arrests and kidnappings in other parts of the country also arrived regularly.

Fanon kept up with his intellectual pursuits as well, writing and presenting scientific papers at specialized congresses, and publishing occasionally. He was appointed FLN's permanent representative in Accra (Ghana) in 1959. Fanon travelled widely, popularizing the Algerian resistance, seeking support and arranging clandestine meetings, and was a speaker at numerous conferences, such as the All-African People's Congress (1958) and Conference of the African Peoples (1960). Fanon possibly survived an assassination attempt when in Rome, in a hospital where he had been admitted after a road accident that damaged his spine and ribs. It was at the Second Congress of Black Writers and Artists (Rome 1959) that Fanon articulated the viewpoint that would eventually become his critique of cultural nationalism. He spoke on 'The Reciprocal Foundation of National Culture and Liberation Struggles' (after Diop and others had praised 'the' black genius!). Here Fanon argued that the nation being a cultural entity, in addition to being a political one, a truly authentic culture has to have a nation as support. Without nations and states, cultures would perish. These arguments would be sharpened and finally appear in *The Wretched of the Earth*. It was also during this time that Fanon was writing the essays that would become *A Dying Colonialism*.

In 1958 the novelist Assia Djebar (b. 1936), who would go on to become one of the key figures of postcolonial Arab and feminist fiction, arrived in Tunis. She met Fanon and wrote propaganda pamphlets for the FLN. Eventually Djebar would become Josie Fanon's close friend. During the 1959–60 period Fanon also published a few essays on his home, Martinique. In one of them, published later in *African* under the title 'Blood Flows in the Antilles Under French Domination', Fanon tried to deal with the bombings in Fort de France. Referring to the events as representing the 'first manifestation of the national spirit of Martinique' (*African*: 169), Fanon assured the revolutionaries of the support of Algerians in their struggle. Meanwhile debates about the right to self-determination for the Algerians raged, and general strikes became the order of the day. Fanon was attending numerous conferences, and travelling to various places to muster support for the Algerian cause, including secret trips to Guinea, Mali, Libya and Liberia. He was also interested in the events unfolding across other African nations – especially the Congo, which had recently acquired independence but was still grappling with political problems. During these trips Fanon was probably collecting information about French troop movements, and considering the logistics of putting together an army to sneak inside Algeria.

During one of these journeys, to Mali, Fanon began to complain of exhaustion. He had lost weight and looked weak. His companions attributed it to his punishing travel schedule. At Accra he condescended to visit a doctor, and tests revealed a huge WBC (white blood corpuscles) count, a symptom of leukaemia. A second visit, this time to a doctor in Tunis, confirmed the bad news: Frantz Fanon had the incurable disease and had, maybe, a year to live. This led to both a medical and an ideological problem in Fanon the revolutionary's life. Medical treatment in African nations, especially for illnesses of this sort, was at best rudimentary. He would have to go to France or the United States. In France he would be either arrested or assassinated, and Fanon, who loathed the US, refused to go there. After considerable negotiations, he agreed to go to Moscow.

The treatment seems to have caused a remission, and Fanon was back to active political work. He may have lectured to the Algerian troops in Tunis around the time he returned from Moscow.

Maybe because he realized that this was only a temporary respite, Fanon was energized enough to travel to meet somebody special. Using his contacts, Fanon finally met Jean-Paul Sartre in Rome in July 1961. Macey records that the two met for lunch and talked till eight the next morning (even though Simone de Beauvoir [1908–86] tried to ensure that Sartre got some sleep!). Fanon is believed to have commented to Charles Lanzmann: 'I don't like people who spare themselves' (Macey 2000: 459).

Fanon was working through the summer of 1961, dictating what would become, after ten months of painful and furious working, his classic *The Wretched of the Earth* (sections of this book would be reprints of Fanon's lectures). The chapter on violence had appeared first in May 1961 in the journal *Les Temps Moderns*, and was revised to fit the book. Sartre's own controversial preface to *Wretched* originally appeared as a 'supplement', inserted into the book as a poster. Fanon did live long enough to see copies of his last book, but the effort of putting together *Wretched* had completely drained him.

During these months of Fanon's composition of *Wretched*, Algeria was everywhere in flames, as violence escalated from both sides. But it was also during these months that a dying Fanon made some of his most prophetic observations – that newly independent societies would lapse into savagery on account of nationalism. As Algeria – indeed other African states as well – would demonstrate less than a decade later, this was to come true. Corruption, ethnicide, xenophobia and fundamentalism would arrive in the late 1980s. Foreigners would be targeted by organizations like the Islamic Salvation Front, intellectuals kidnapped and executed, all dissent silenced.

After persistent refusals to go to the country he detested, Fanon conceded and eventually was taken to the USA in October 1961. Enroute to the USA, they had a stopover in Rome, and Sartre visited Fanon at his hotel. On 3 October 1961 Fanon arrived in Washington, D.C.

Numerous conspiracy theories circulate about Fanon's death – about how he was kept in a hotel room in Washington, D.C. for eight days and not taken to a hospital for treatment because the CIA wanted to interrogate him. (The CIA had been involved in getting Fanon into the USA.) By the time Fanon reached the hospital, the National Institute of Health, Bethesda, Maryland, he was in the last stages. He received a blood transfusion eventually, a desperate attempt to restore his blood cells, but it was already too late. In his last moments, Fanon did see the first reviews of *Wretched*, the book that would go on to become the bible of revolutionaries around the world.

Frantz Fanon died on 6 December 1961 from double pneumonia. He was 36 at the time. Charles Lanzmann records:

> Fanon lived his death minute by minute and had resisted it savagely; his prickly aggressivity found a release in the fantasies of a dying man: he hated those American racists, and distrusted hospital staff.
>
> (quoted in Macey 2000: 490–1)

His body was smuggled back into Algeria – the country whose revolution Fanon analyzed and documented with such a passionate intensity – and buried in the FLN cemetery. On 3 July 1962, a few months after Fanon's death, Algeria became independent.

The first detailed biographies emerged in the 1970s (Caute 1970, Geismer 1971 and Gendzier 1973), and commentaries emerged around the same time. Josie Fanon, who watched Algerians turn against each other in the late 1980s just as Fanon predicted, is believed to have phoned her friend Assia Djebar (once Fanon's colleague and now a well-known novelist and film-maker), to sorrowfully exclaim: 'the wretched of the earth again'. Josie Fanon committed suicide in 1989. A literary prize, Prix Frantz Fanon, was established in Martinique in 1987.

SUMMARY

Fanon's life was rooted in two key contexts: his work as a doctor and his work as an active member of the revolutionary forces. As we shall see in the explication of his writings, both of these contexts informed his ideas about colonial rule (especially colonial biomedicine), the colonial subject psyche (especially the dependency complex and the tendency to violence), the nature of the anti-colonial struggle, and the tensions and dynamics of nationalism.

2

INFLUENCES AND ENGAGEMENTS

Fanon was an extraordinarily eclectic thinker. As we now know, he had been a voracious reader during childhood, and as a medical student and psychiatrist he had read more in philosophy than in his chosen discipline. This chapter indicates the nature of Fanon's influences, tracing some of his intellectual lineages, from French existentialist philosopher and novelist Jean-Paul Sartre (1905–80) through Aimé Césaire (1913–2008), the founder of psychoanalysis Sigmund Freud (1856–1939) and the French psychoanalyst Jacques Lacan (1901–81).

While Césaire's was an influence that Fanon openly admitted to, there were several others as well – from the existential phenomenology of Jean-Paul Sartre through Marxism and Lacanian psychoanalysis to Mannoni and Césaire. Udo Krautwurst (2003) has demonstrated how Fanon's definitions of colonialism, colonial subjects and subjectivities show remarkable parallels with poststructuralist ideas. Thus when Fanon announces that the colonist derives his 'validity' from the 'colonial system' (*Wretched:* 2), he is, in Krautwurst's reading, arguing that colonial discourse constructs subjects such as natives and colonial masters. Other critics have argued, not very convincingly, one must say, that various strands of Fanon's revolutionary theory came from Islamic traditions of anti-colonial struggle, even though Fanon does not reference this influence or tradition explicitly (see Slisli 2008).

Eclectic, intellectually agile, but always radical in his reinterpretation of these thinkers, Fanon never hesitated to critique any/all of them. Grounding his philosophical meditations in his very material conditions of psychiatric training, Martinique, Algeria and hospital life enabled Fanon to constantly position 'theory' within 'practice'. Observing the FLN and the anti-colonial struggles from close quarters and as a participating activist was important to Fanon's thinking through the questions of nationalism and decolonization, just as his encounters with black patients with psychological problems enabled him to interrogate Freud's theories about the supposedly universal Oedipal complex. Describing his work as 'social psychiatry' (Bulhan 1985) draws our attention to the embeddedness of psychiatric 'theory' within praxis in Fanon where he constantly grounded his analysis of psychotic conditions in the social and material contexts of the blacks, or the colonized.

What must be kept in mind is that Fanon never accepted any philosophical thought or thinker uncritically. He appropriates Sartre's idea of relational identity, but critiques Sartre as well. Likewise, he admires Césaire and accepts the immediate (or short-term) necessity of negritude, but also offers a deeply thought out response where he rejects particular strands of both Césaire and negritude, especially for their long-term impact. This is precisely why 'Fanon's influences' become such a difficult subject – we do not see Fanon's appropriation of a thinker, what we see is a critical engagement, an engagement that very often indicts the shortcomings and politics of the thinker and extends the ideas into a wholly other dimension. Thus Fanon's reading of Sartre starts off with Sartrean existentialism and the debate over an existential identity. But Fanon then extends this to develop an existential ethics where difference is recognized and respected, and can form the basis of a new humanism that is beyond white and black. In his engagement with Césaire, Fanon accepts negritude and its cultural nationalism as necessary, but proposes that this can only be an early stage in the anti-colonial struggle. Finally, in the case of psychoanalysis, Fanon engages with ideas of psychosis and the inferiority complex but only to claim that these are not individual conditions. In the case of blacks, he argues, psychoanalysis does not quite explain the problems because the complexes and disorders are embedded not in the individual psyche but in the social and economic contexts.

The focus in this chapter is Fanon's appropriation of four key influences in his work:

- Aimé Césaire and negritude;
- Marxism;
- Sartre and existentialism;
- Psychoanalysis.

AIMÉ CÉSAIRE AND NEGRITUDE

There are direct echoes of Aimé Césaire throughout Fanon's work. The Introduction to *Black Skin* pays homage to Césaire's influence on Fanon in the form of the epigraph: 'I am talking of millions of men who have been skilfully injected with fear, inferiority complexes, trepidation, servility, despair, abasement' (from Césaire's *Discourse on Colonialism*, cited in *Black Skin*: 1). Later in the same work Fanon declares: 'It was only with the appearance of Aimé Césaire that the acceptance of negritude and the statement of its claims began to be perceptible' (118). When Fanon refers to Nazi Germany's near-colonization of Europe in *Black Skin* (66–7) he quotes Césaire's *Discourse on Colonialism* where Césaire describes how Hitler applied to the whole of Europe colonialist practices previously used against Arabs, Indian coolies and American blacks. Fanon would refer to the Nazis' 'enslavement' of European groups as the 'institution of a colonial system in the very heart of Europe' in his 'Racism and Culture' (*African*: 33). Beyond these direct echoes and quotes, Fanon's work shows Césaire's influence in several arguments.

Black Skin is Fanon's most Césairean work, and has even been interpreted as a rewriting of Césaire's 1939 *Notebook of a Return to My Native Land* (Wilder 2004: 39). In his essay 'West Indians and Africans' (*African*) Fanon claims that Césaire was the first to show him that 'it is fine and good to be a Negro' (*African*: 21). Negritude, as Césaire saw it, was an attempt to restore pride in (i) black identity and (ii) black cultural practices. Often associated with the term 'black consciousness', it served an important purpose in anti-colonial struggles in Africa: it enabled the unification of Africans under a common label, and it enabled the retrieval of cultural practices and memories that colonialism had erased. Fanon, like Césaire, saw this movement as useful, for it could serve, he believed, the greater cause of African consciousness which had been sealed off by colonial consciousness.

Negritude was a cultural movement within the anti-colonial struggles of African nations. It called for a return to native ways of thinking, belief and cultural practices. Thus mysticism, native forms of music and arts, and spiritualism were revived. The larger aim was to retrieve the pride of being black and a 'black consciousness'.

It is also from Césaire that Fanon borrows his incredulity towards negritude's retreat into the past at the cost of the present. Césaire was sceptical about the valorization of a past that had already been described as perverse by the whites – and already contaminated by colonial cultures. In other words, Césaire was doubtful of the entire project of retrieving a *pure* native past that would (i) not be mere exoticising, (ii) nativist and (iii) already contaminated (Wilder 2004: 41). But he was emphatic, like Fanon after him, that the search for the mythical golden past in no way alleviated the miseries of the present (for the natives). Nativism, for both Césaire and Fanon, was not really the answer to colonialism.

Fanon did find negritude as possessing considerable political relevance in the anti-colonial struggle. In his essay 'West Indians and Africans' (*African*) Fanon noted that political consciousness comes to the West Indian through negritude. Here Fanon adopts Césaire's and other negritude writers' celebration of African culture (the 'rhythms'), as well as rhetoric and images (see Bernasconi 2002). Fanon's critique of negritude (as we shall see in a later chapter) targeted its:

- essentialism, rejecting an idea of 'the' African culture, as if it was pure and monolithic;
- temporality, rejecting any idea of the African *past*, as if there is any pre-colonial pure African past.

He turned away from Césaire and negritude primarily in his efforts to transcend essentialisms of every kind. Fanon's rejection of negritude finds its strongest expression in his (now-cult) essay 'On National Culture' in *Wretched*.

First, he did not want to be tied down to an African or black past alone: he wanted to 'recapture the whole past of the world' (*Wretched*: 176). With this he rejects one of negritude's central assumptions – that decolonization must be accompanied by a retrieval of the African past. The African, Fanon argues, must refuse to be 'sealed away' in the 'Tower of the Past' (a phrase he takes from Césaire; *Black Skin*: 176).

Second, Fanon emphasized that his sympathies were not only with Africans fighting for dignity and independence but with any/all oppressed peoples. It is not a coincidence that his work is titled *Wretched of the Earth*, and not *Wretched of Africa*. He writes as early as *Black Skin*: 'Every time a man has contributed to the victory of the dignity of the spirit, every time a man has said no to an attempt to subjugate his fellows, I have felt solidarity with his act' (176).

Third, Fanon was wary of the negritude discourse of *the* Negro. As he would argue in 'West Indians and Africans', there is 'nothing, *a priori*, to warrant the assumption that a Negro people exist' (*African*: 18). Césaire's and negritude's valorization of an essential black identity, according to Fanon's critique (where he turns away from Césaire), results in a 'black hole' where all blacks are lumped together irrespective of historical and cultural differences (27).

What emerges in Fanon's engagement with Césaire is his (Fanon's) emphasis on the respect for difference – among Africans themselves. While Césaire saw advantages to a unified African identity and cultural nationalism, Fanon was far more cautious. Fanon anticipated the xenophobic ethnicide of the 1990s in Rwanda, Sudan and other African nations. He was also clear-sighted enough to see cultural nationalism as swerving into nativism – the excessive pride in native traditions and native culture, which posits a fear and dislike of 'foreign' culture – and murderous tribalisms. Fanon attempts to make a difficult but necessary shift from universalizing tendencies – negritude's emphasis on 'the' black identity – to a respect for particulars with his emphasis on difference.

MARXISM

A Dying Colonialism's last chapter was in honour of Marx's *18th Brumaire*. In *Black Skin* (174) Fanon had quoted from this text of Marx, though there are references to Sartre's Marxism elsewhere. Fanon tried to use Marxian theories to evolve a theory of the revolutionary class – the class that would overthrow the social order and the capitalist regime. While this component of Marxism is visible in all of

Fanon, his appropriation of other aspects of Marxist thought are open to question.

Fanon remained more or less contemptuous of the Algerian and French left, especially as it manifest in the Algerian Communist Party (which he saw as reformist and weak). His debts to Marxism have always been the matter of considerable dispute (Martin 1970; Woddis 1972; Wallerstein 1979: 250–67; Macey 2000: 478–82). Part of the problem is with Fanon's Marxist terminology, which was sometimes confusing. When, for instance, he described the 'peasantry' as 'revolutionary', it shocked Marxists around the world (Wallerstein 1979: 257–8). However, the 'peasantry' that Fanon was describing was not the wealthy peasant but a poor, perhaps landless one who might end up becoming a wage labourer (Wallerstein 1979: 258).

Fanon was firmly convinced, after Marx, that the class distinctions and differences in Algerian society were the creation of colonial domination and exploitation. His new humanism itself might have Marxist roots, coming to Fanon via Sartre's *Critique of Dialectical Reason* which read Marx's 1844 text, *Economic-Philosophic Manuscripts* (Bernasconi 1996), where both Marx and Sartre see revolution as resulting in a 'positive humanism' (Sartre's term).

Fanon also firmly believed that class struggle was an integral component of freedom struggles in African, and that the peasants were the true revolutionary class. Suspicious of the nationalist bourgeois, Fanon saw them as collaborating with the colonial structures. Such a bourgeois would accumulate capital, believed Fanon. Here Fanon rejects the traditional Marxist role of the proletariat as well.

He therefore consistently underscored the class dimension of liberation struggles and the racialized capitalist colonialism. The *lumpenproletariat* (the pimps, hooligans, unemployed), for Fanon, is the only true revolutionary class because this class alone had 'spontaneity', whereas the intelligentsia has been too sold on western ideas. Fanon thus rejects the traditional category of the proletariat and instead treats the *lumpenproletariat* and the peasantry as truly revolutionary. The *lumpenproletariat* is, in Wallerstein's definition, made of semi-proletarians, who earn one part of their life-income from wage labour and the other part from sources such as state dole or theft. They are only semi-employed and therefore are more exploited and truly the wretched of the earth – and the group most likely to erupt into violence (Wallerstein 1979: 264–5).

SARTRE AND EXISTENTIALISM

One of Fanon's lasting influences was phenomenology and existentialism. When still a student at Fort de France and later Lyon he had read extensively in Sartre, especially *Les Temps Modernes*. At Lyon he had attended the lectures of French phenomenologist philosopher Maurice Merleau-Ponty (1908–61).

Sartre posited the social contexts of consciousness. He emphasized *lived experience* as foundational to identity. In the great phenomenology texts of the time, Merleau-Ponty's *The Phenomenology of Perception* (1945) and Sartre's works, Fanon found the philosophical grounding he needed to analyse identity in the colonial context. Fanon proposes that the black colonized has no history, and no humanness left to him. This is essentially an existential argument that Fanon is running, but via what he calls a 'socio-diagnostic'. Colonialism denies the very Being of blackness, and thus denies him an existential identity. Fanon found this a useful framework in which to analyse the development (or rather, non-development) of the black man's identity: the lived experience of racism and colonialism ensures that the black man would only see and experience himself as an object reduced to a 'thingness' by the non-recognition of the whites.

Sartre had argued in his *Anti-Semite and Jew* (1965) that the anti-Semite *made* the Jew. Sartre would write: 'By treating the Jew as an inferior and pernicious being, I affirm at the same time I belong to the elite' (quoted in *Black Skin*: 64). In other words, Sartre was proposing a *relational* view of identity. The Other was necessary to me because I am validated by the Other, in this view. Here the anti-Semite is able to demonstrate his superiority only be portraying the Jew as inferior. For Fanon this was a useful theoretical frame in which to read colonial relations. Note the opening of *Black Skin* where Fanon would state that we need to understand the black man's 'comprehension of the dimension *of the Other*' (8, emphasis in original). Fanon would then go on to propose that the very identity of the colonized native was dependent upon (i) the colonial relation of master–slave and (ii) the colonial master's construction of the colonized as savage. It is the White who constructs the Black in the colonial situation. Fanon thus argued that the native's inferiority complex was the 'correlative' to the European's feelings of superiority (*Black Skin*: 69). The racist, Fanon writes, 'creates his inferior' (69).

Fanon's discovery of self-hate and self-revulsion for being black is akin to Sartre's idea of nausea (Ahluwalia 2003). In the famous scene recounted to us in *Black Skin*, Fanon tells us how, when the young child in Paris points out his skin colour ('Look, a Negro', 84), he is made *aware* of his blackness. 'I took myself far off' (85). He then goes on: 'What else could it be for me but an amputation, an excision, a hemorrhage that spattered my whole body with black blood' (85). Ahluwalia, rightly I think, suggests that Fanon here is 'disempowered by nausea to the recognition of being trapped, injured and most importantly of the possibility to break out of that condition' (Ahluwalia 2003: 344–5). Ahluwalia sees Fanon's description of his existential crisis as directly echoing Sartre's notion of nausea. Nausea is the realization of one's racial identity, but also a realization that this racial identity is a source of trauma, shame and oppression. It is the intense self-dislike that is born out of this realization.

Sartre's notion of existential freedom as central to identity is woven into Fanon's rejection of negritude as well. It is the human's destiny, writes Fanon, to 'be set free' (*Black Skin*). While negritude sought an essential black identity, and debates about reparations (for the slavery Africans suffered) were underway, Fanon rejected both claims outright. To seek reparations, Fanon argued, was to remain trapped forever in the past and the identity of the 'slave'. Later, in *Wretched*, however, Fanon was to argue a case for reparations (see Chapter 7). To 'exist absolutely', he argues, is to deny the right to 'lock away' the identity of the self within such 'retroactive reparations' (*Black Skin*: 180). Fanon's (existential) emphasis on radical freedom, taken, I suggest, from Sartre, is what makes him depart from negritude and Césaire. There is no essential blackness, just as there is no essential whiteness – 'the Negro is not. Any more than the white man', writes Fanon (180).

Sartre proposed that negritude was a 'weak stage' in the evolution of black identity. He proposes a 'dialectical progression', where black marches ahead *only* in relation to the white (dialectic is the binary linkage of two terms, in this case 'black *and* white'). While Sartre praises the poetry of negritude as revolutionary, the very idea of negritude, Sartre writes in *Black Orpheus* (1948), reinstates the white as the positive term in the dialectic, and black as its *negative* term. But this 'weak moment', Sartre proposes, is not an end, just a *means*. Negritude must serve the cause of the end of racism by destroying itself. Thus Sartre reinforced a hierarchy – white over black – when he proposed this dialectic as a route to anti-racist synthesis. Fanon responded to this argument with considerable horror and anger in *Black Skin*. He denied any revolutionary scope to the poetry of negritude. Rather than being revolutionary, the poetry glorified a 'mummified' past, converting it into an exotic commodity. Fanon thus rejects Sartre's rehabilitation of native/black culture as a 'banal quest for the exotic' (*Wretched*: 158).

Recognizing the dialectic's dubious argument about hierarchic terms, Fanon mourned that '[he] had been robbed of [his] last chance' because 'black' was only a minor term in Sartre's dialectic (*Black Skin*: 102, 106). Despite this irritation with Sartre's views, towards the end of *Black Skin*, Fanon himself has begun to see the inadequacies of negritude's anti-racist racism. Thus when he rejects the exaltation of the past in negritude, he has effectively come around to Sartre's way of thinking.

Sartre's existential ethics were also to influence Fanon (Haddour 2005). Sartre seeks assimilation within the nation-state based on an ethics of *difference*, where difference is respected. That is, in any nation-state blacks, Jews and whites would be together while *retaining* their differences. A nation-state respects difference, in Sartre's scheme. This line of thought – about the respect for and an ethics of difference – would be something that Fanon would retain in his critique of negritude and Césaire as well. Fanon turns Sartre towards a new humanism that is based on this very ethics of difference. Just as the Jew cannot be assimilated without a true openness to difference the black cannot be integrated into the life of a nation without first being allowed his existential identity, even if that identity is 'different'. Haddour points out that Fanon's humanism is *not* the western humanism inherited from the eighteenth-century Enlightenment – which was complicit with colonialism. Neither does it encourage the essentialisms of negritude (Haddour 2005: 300). 'I find myself suddenly in the world and I recognize that I have one right alone: That of demanding human behavior from the other', writes Fanon (*Black Skin*: 179). The sense of self-hood, often called 'subjectivity', cannot be entirely dependent upon one-self. Individuals develop a sense of self only in relation with other selves, other individuals in society. I am I because I am *not* you, in my *difference* from you. So in order to have a sense of 'I' it needs a 'you'. You have to recognize me, acknowledge me as different, therein lies my sense of self. In other words, subjectivity, as Fanon proposes following

Sartre, and the existentialists discover, is *intersubjectivity*. What Fanon's existential humanism does is to cultivate an (perhaps utopian) ideal of a universalism based on difference, of mutual recognition and the decolonization of both the colonizer and the colonized.

Fanon's espousal of violence as an agential act for the colonized to gain subjectivity and identity may also have been drawn from Sartre. Sartre argued (in *Critique of Dialectical Reason*) that violence occurs because people have been alienated from the lived realities of society. Towards the end of his Preface to Fanon's *Wretched*, Sartre presented violence as an act of agency on the part of the oppressed and the condemned. This, as Neil Roberts has noted (2004), is the same stance that Fanon takes towards violence. Colonialism which brutalizes the colonized so that he has no subjectivity left drives the native to violence as a means of regaining subjectivity.

PSYCHOANALYSIS

Fanon effectively harnessed psychoanalysis to explain the supposed inferiority complex, violence and neuroses of the colonized. Freud, the Swiss psychoanalyst C. G. Jung (1875–1961), the Austrian doctor Alfred Adler (1870–1937), the French psychoanalyst Octave Mannoni (1899–1989) and Lacan all figure in Fanon's work, but each is subject to critical scrutiny.

Freud famously proposed that neurosis springs from (i) incestuous fantasies, (ii) the Oedipal complex and (iii) sexual abuse in childhood.

> The Oedipal complex was Sigmund Freud's famous theorization of the male child's love for his mother that results in a hatred of the father, whom the child sees as a rival for the mother. It derives from Sophocles' Greek play about the hero Oedipus who married his mother Jocasta, though without being aware of the nature of his true relationship to her.

Thus Freudian psychoanalytic theory situated the causes of neurosis and trauma within the *individual*. Freud also locates all neurosis within the *family*. Fanon takes issue with Freud in this individualization of trauma.

Fanon claims that Freud locates all psychological problems in the *individual* psyche. Traditional (European) psychoanalysis does not adequately explain the *black*'s situation and inferiority complex: 'the black man's alienation is not an individual question' (*Black Skin*: 4). Fanon consciously situates psychiatric problems and psychiatric practice within a social and economic context. What he calls a 'socio-diagnostic' is the psychoanalytic framework recast to account for these contexts. Thus he is able to declare with great certainty that 'there is nothing psychotic in the Blacks' (43) because the neurosis and psychosis proceed from the social conditions that alienate the black. There is no route for the black man's catharsis, since he has (i) been denied any subjectivity within colonialism and (ii) assimilated the white man's image of himself.

Fanon summarily rejects the psychoanalytic framework of the Oedipal complex. In *Black Skin*, in a footnote, he records his disagreement with 'Dr Lacan' who, says Fanon, 'talks of the "abundance" of the Oedipus complex' (117, fn 14). As Fanon famously puts it, 97 per cent of the families in the Antilles would not be able to show even a single Oedipal complex (117). The Oedipal, Fanon argues, holds little theoretical relevance because the individual psyche and values are intimately linked to both nation and family in the case of Africa. Once again, Fanon shifts the debate out of the individual psyche into the social domain. The Oedipal is not, in the case of the Africans, rooted in the family (as Freud famously proposed), but in the social.

Fanon's next major disagreement with psychoanalysis occurs in his critique, in *Black Skin*, of Octave Mannoni's psychoanalysis in his *Prospero and Caliban: The Psychology of Colonization* (1950, English translation 1964). Mannoni had famously theorized a 'dependency complex' of the blacks in the colonial encounter. Mannoni proposed:

1 that the colonial situation could be read as an encounter between the civilized and the savage;
2 that an inferiority complex, based on the colour of one's skin, is natural when that individual belongs to a minority group within a larger group;
3 that the black man with his inferiority complex feels secure only when he enters into a dependency relationship with the white man.

Fanon responds to these (white) psychoanalytic readings of race methodically. He notes that the white man is numerically a minority in Africa (two hundred whites as opposed to three hundred thousand black Martinicans), yet they do not see themselves as inferior. Instead, notes Fanon, these two hundred see themselves as superior to the majority (*Black Skin*: 68). Fanon argues that in the colonial situation the black man is robbed of his worth, dignity and self. He is reduced to a 'parasite', a 'brute beast', a 'walking dung-heap' (73). All 'psychological mechanisms' of the native are destroyed, writes Fanon (72). The white man acts from a social and political (and not psychological) position of authority, argues Fanon.

Fanon then rejects Mannoni's thesis of personality types (the 'dependent' native type and the 'authoritarian' European type). Dependency and inferiority complexes are not the consequence of any flaw in the black man's mental make-up, as Mannoni's analysis suggests. The white man is looked up to by the black man not because the white man is inherently superior and the black inherently dependent, but because the colonial situation creates this relationship through threats and violence. These types and complexes emerge because of the inequalities of the races in the colonial context. They emerge from the horrific economic, political and social contexts of the black man's life under colonization. As we shall see in the chapter on race and psychoanalysis, Fanon was keen on showing the material bases of the black man's psychological troubles.

Using these arguments about 'dependency' Mannoni analysed the 1947 rebellion as the result of a psychological collapse in the black people: feeling abandoned by the white masters whom they had come to trust, they took to violence. Mannoni called it 'childish rage'. Fanon finds this interpretation, which treats all violence as intrinsic to the African's character, problematic. The rebellion, Fanon argues, was the consequence of a systematic undermining of the African's sense of selfhood, of the nationalist upsurge among them, and the slow recognition of the unequal nature of racial relations among Africans.

In another psychoanalytic interpretation, Mannoni argued that when the native, black man dreams of guns, they are essentially phallic images. Fanon is outraged at this interpretation of the gun as a mere symbol. One cannot see only symbolism when the threat is very real, he believed. Fanon argued that the rifle in the hands of the colonized (in his dreams) is no Freudian symbol, or phallic metaphor – it is a *real* rifle he is dreaming of and one which can injure the black body (*Black Skin*: 79). One cannot lose sight of the real and be trapped within such fancy symbolism.

Fanon in his essay 'The Man of Color and the White Woman' (*Black Skin*) reads the notorious (alleged) desire of the black man for the white woman not in psychoanalytic terms alone, but in social terms. The black man, alienated from his own culture and self, now sees himself through the white man's eyes. He craves the white man's recognition not as a black man but as equally *white* (*Black Skin*: 45). This desire to be recognized as white leads the black man to see the white woman as a means to acquire this recognition. The black man thus seeks to 'marry White culture, White beauty, White Whiteness' (45). It is not the woman *per se* that the black desires, it is 'white civilization and dignity' (45). That is, the white woman, in Fanon's gendered reading, is a means to an end, directed towards the end of becoming white.

Fanon's critique of colonialism does take, as we can see, psychoanalytic overtones. Armed with a psychoanalytic framework, Fanon is able to argue that the colonized black internalizes the white man's desires and paranoias. The blacks do possess some form of the 'collective unconscious' (Jung also figures in Fanon's analysis), but this unconscious is the repository of the repressed desires of the blacks as well as that of the whites. The European's own repressed desires for the blacks have to be doubly repressed by the blacks, since they have internalized the white man's perspectives.

Fanon refuses to privilege the unconscious or the individual psyche over the social. Thus in *Wretched*, while retaining the psychoanalytic framework, Fanon moves his grounds of analysis to a more political level, even when discussing consciousness. What is crucial in Fanon is his insistence that psychoanalysis at best offers only a partial explanation for psychiatric problems. He further demonstrates that psychoanalysis is only interested in the individual psyche. But in the case of the African and the colonized, psychiatric disorders and neuroses are never solely individual in origin. These are socially induced, by the conditions of oppression and alienation, which is colonialism. As critics have argued, Fanon exhibits a constant move from the psychological to the political and vice versa (McCullough 1983; Lebeau 1998; Hook 2005).

Fanon recognized the material consequences of the dependency complex – sickness and violence among the colonial subjects – and thus moved away from Mannoni's dangerous essentialism about the inherently dependent nature of the black man. He was one of the first to theorize the nature of the colonial subject's violence as originating in the social, material and psychological conditions of colonialism.

Indeed, as Derek Hook observes, Fanon's psychology links 'the domain of psychological action to a world of concrete and material effects' (Hook 2005: 482).

SUMMARY

Four key intellectual origins of Fanon's complex work and thought might be traced, as this chapter has done. Aimé Césaire's idea of negritude and the black man's pride in black culture struck Fanon as at once necessary and dangerous. Essential, because it would help retrieve a cultural tradition that has been eroded, even erased, by the colonial master's culture; dangerous, because Fanon saw it as essentialist, seeking a 'pure' African past where none existed – an essentialism that would, in Fanon's view, lead to xenophobic nationalism. From Marxism Fanon adapted the idea of class struggle. He attributed the class distinctions and differences in Algerian society to the structures and processes of colonial rule. For Fanon the organization of the peasants as the true revolutionary class was central to the anti-colonial struggle. This focus on the peasant class as the key constituent of the revolutionary struggle was premised on Fanon's suspicion of the nationalist bourgeois, which he saw as collaborating with the colonial structures. Through his engagement with Sartre's phenomenology and existential thought, Fanon elaborated a theory of the colonial subject's psyche. Colonialism, Fanon proposed, denies the very Being of the black man: the black man had no existential identity. The lived experience of racism and colonialism ensured that the black man would only see and experience himself as an object reduced to a 'thingness' by non-recognition by the whites, never as a full consciousness or Being. Since subjectivity (or selfhood) develops only in relation with other selves, other individuals in society, colonialism's non-recognition of the black meant that the black would not develop a clear subjectivity. Finally, adapting ideas from psychoanalysis, Fanon argued that the famous 'dependency complex' (a theory popularized by Mannoni about colonized races) was the product not of the black mind but of the colonial situation. The helpless colonized black internalizes the white man's desires and fears; he sees himself through the white man's eyes. The African's psychiatric disorders and neuroses are not individual in origin but social, rooted in the horrific life he leads under colonial rule. Fanon thus displaced the individual-centric theories of psychoanalysis in favour of a 'socio-diagnostic' (his term) of African mental illness.

3

COLONIALISM, RACE AND THE NATIVE PSYCHE

In *Wide Sargasso Sea* (1966), Dominican novelist Jean Rhys' (1890–1979) rewriting of the English literary classic, Charlotte Brontë's *Jane Eyre* (1847), Antoinette (the first Mrs Rochester) is rejected by her husband because of her problematic racial identity; she is Creole (Rhys herself had a Welsh father and a Creole mother). As their marriage disintegrates, Antoinette finds herself isolated and eventually goes mad. Rhys' novel maps the slow descent: from the initial exotic appeal of a person of mixed heritage to her eventual humiliation at the hands of a race-conscious colonial society. *Wide Sargasso Sea* is an emblematic text for a particularly horrific consequence of colonial rule: the madness of the colonized. It is this consequence of colonial rule that occupied Frantz Fanon for a considerable amount of time, as both practising psychiatrist and social theorist.

This chapter examines Fanon's psychoanalysis of the racial encounter and his concerns with:

- race, colonialism and identity;
- the black man's inferiority complex and race;
- the Dependency Complex;
- 'mental disorders' and colonial psychiatry.

Fanon's psychoanalysis was not merely a teasing out of the unconscious drives and instincts of the black psyche. Rather, his focus was always on the social conditions in which psychic disorders were produced. In *Black Skin* Fanon spoke of the 'arsenal of complexes' produced by the colonial environment (19). Colonialism, for Fanon, is inherently 'psychopathological' (Vaughan 1993: 47), producing great mental disturbances in both colonizer and colonized. Fanon arrived at this conclusion through his psychiatric practice and treatment of patients in Algeria. His work is therefore replete with examples of patients and he cites case histories to demonstrate his arguments.

Fanon admitted to the role of the unconscious or the drives, and was certain that only psychoanalytic interpretations could reveal the inferiority complex in the black man (*Black Skin*: 3). But he also recognized that western psychiatric and psychoanalytic paradigms – he critiques Sigmund Freud, C. G. Jung, Adler, O. Mannoni and Jacques Lacan in his writings – did not apply easily to African cultures or individuals. Fanon firmly believed that neurosis, psychiatric disorders or aggression were induced by social factors and contexts rather than simply psychological factors (*Black Skin*: 4). He thus roots the *psychological* in the *material* context. Neurosis, aggression or psychiatric disorders among the colonized blacks could not be attributed, Fanon argued, to the Oedipal complex because the very interpretive frame of the Oedipal was Euro-American. Fanon claimed that in the French Antilles, 97 per cent of the families would not exhibit even one Oedipal neurosis (*Black Skin*: 117).

Fanon's major contribution to the psychoanalysis of the racial encounter is elaborated in his claim that 'every neurosis, every abnormal manifestation' in the Antillean was a result of his (racialized) cultural situation (*Black Skin*: 117–18). This is Fanon's 'social psychiatry' (Bulhan 1985), which argues that human psychology is embedded in the cultural and socio-historical context.

RACE, COLONIALISM AND IDENTITY

Psychoanalysis helped Fanon formulate theories of black identity in the colonial situation. Fanon argues the following:

- All identity is relational, where the Self can understand its identity only in relation to the Other, or another.
- In the colonial context the black man only sees himself as the negative to/of the white man.

- White is the norm, and black the deviation from the norm.
- The black man only sees himself as an object, with no sense of the Self because the white man only sees him as an object.
- To escape from the condition of being mere object, the black man seeks to *become* white: he craves recognition from the white man.
- Thus there is no self-recognition, no self-awareness in the black man in the colonial situation.

Fanon begins with the idea that the black man is only the other (with the 'o' in lower case to distinguish it from the *Other*) to the white man. This condition where the Self is denied selfhood reduces the black man to an *object* rather than a human being (*Black Skin*: 82). For the black his self is simply an object 'in the midst of other objects' (82). The black man lacks an identity because he constantly seeks affirmation from the white, *as* white – which, of course, he never will be.

Man, argues Fanon in his essay, 'The Negro and Hegel', acquires a sense of self or self-worth through the validating gaze of the other. Every self seeks to create a sense of the self in the reciprocal gaze: I see you, and you see me. But when this gaze is absent or denied, as is the case in colonialism, then a conflict arises.

The white man does not seek validation from the black man. Instead, when faced with the black man, the white finds his identity threatened because the fantasy, or image, of the black man as cannibal, rapist and murderer intervenes. 'Whoever says *rape* says *Negro*', writes Fanon (*Black Skin*: 127, emphasis in original). This fantasy is the white race's collective unconscious around and about the black man (for the white woman, of course, the black man represents unbridled sexuality: the black man symbolizes biology and the penis, as Fanon sees it, *Black Skin:* 128). That is, for the white race, the black man is *reducible* to sexuality. When faced with a black man the white mind jumps immediately to ideas about the entire black race's rampant sexuality – a theme that has figured in much colonial writing on Asia and Africa.

Thus the 'rape' of Adela Quested in *Passage to India* (1924), English novelist E. M. Forster's (1879–1970) paradigmatic text for postcolonial studies, retrieves the nineteenth-century colonial anxiety of the rape of the white woman by the hyper-sexual black/brown man (for studies, see Jenny Sharpe 1993 and Nancy Paxton 1999). The entire British community in the small Indian town of Chandrapore is in uproar because the English woman has been allegedly dishonoured and abused. This 'act' therefore serves as a synecdoche, in the British imagination, of the dishonour of the Empire and Britain itself. In English novelist Paul Scott's (1920–78) epic, *The Raj Quartet* (1966–75), it is again the rape of the white woman by anonymous Indian men that triggers the violence (primarily retribution by the British police against the Indians). The affair of the white Mary with the black Moses in British-Rhodesian novelist Doris Lessing's *The Grass is Singing* (1950) recalls the theme in a slightly different way (Lessing was born of British parents in Persia/ Iran, and grew up in Rhodesia, now Zimbabwe). The *woman*'s sexuality remains the site where issues of racial identities and national pride are contested (Sharpe 1993; Paxton 1999; McClintock 1995). Fanon, like many of these writers, therefore draws our attention to the *sexualized* nature of all racial relations in the colonial context.

The white man, in Fanon's reading, does not require the validation of the black man's gaze: he is self-contained and self-identical ('I AM white'). The white man becomes the master because he does not need the reciprocating gaze. The black man who sees himself only as 'NOT white', requires recognition, and thus becomes a *thing*. Thus colonialism's psychology, in Fanon's reading, has a double layer:

- All recognition belongs to the white master, who is empowered to recognize and to grant recognition.
- The slave yearns and strives for this recognition from the white master.

Subjectivity, the sense of self, is the privilege and prerogative of the white man alone in this colonial context. This destroys any chance of identity-formation for the black man. In the European's non-reciprocating gaze the black man is merely an object. The black is excluded from the very category of the human. He is less-than-human, an object. Even his labour does not fetch him (the slave) recognition. Due to this craving for recognition, to escape the condition of being only a negative cipher or object, the black man is forced to absorb features of the white master.

He has to constantly mime the colonizer. The colonized hopes to be *like*, and therefore *liked by*, the colonizer. It is only in mimicry that the colonized reinforces his status as colonized: perpetually condemned to just mimic. Thus the black aims to speak a different linguistic register, claims to be 'brown' rather than 'black', Martinican rather than African. Fanon says he is 'astonished' to hear blacks trying to use a different register, what he calls 'putting on the white world' (*Black Skin*: 23). The black man, argues Fanon, wants to 'turn White or disappear' (xxxiii). In other words, he seeks to deracinate himself, lose his colour, his language and his very identity, by mimicking the white 'masters'. Let us take a couple of literary examples where we can see this theme of colonial mimicry in operation.

Indian novelist Attia Hosain (1913–98) describes an Indian woman, Mrs Perin Wadia, as being 'prouder of Western culture than those who were born into it', in her novel, *Sunlight on a Broken Column* (1988 [1961]: 32). Hosain is describing a mimicry, a deracination (the term used to describe the slow voluntary 'erosion' of racial characteristics) that erases the identity of the native, both in terms of an individual as well as in terms of a culture. The native aspires to be accepted by the colonial master through an appropriation of western manners of speech, behaviour and attitudes.

Nigerian playwright, essayist and poet Wole Soyinka (b. 1934) satirizes the native/colonized's desire to speak, look and act as the white master in a truly tragic-comic scene in *Death and the King's Horseman*. The Yoruba women are mimicking Englishmen's speeches in order to mock Amusa, a Yoruba who has joined the police force and tries to behave like his white masters. The Yoruba women aim to bring home to him through this little charade-masquerade how absurd the mimicry is.

> Your invitation card please,
> Who are you? Have we been introduced?
> And who did you say you were?
> Sorry, I didn't quite catch your name.
> May I take your hat?
> If you insist. May I take yours?
>
> (1984: 177–8)

Amusa is, of course, enraged.

In a different but related sense, Caribbean author Jamaica Kincaid (b. 1949) in *A Small Place* expresses her anger at the dominance of English, a language that reminds her of her past:

> Isn't it odd that the only language I have in which to speak of this crime [colonialism] is the language of the criminal who committed the crime?
>
> (1988: 31)

However, despite his mimicry and impersonation, the native is doomed to fail: the very acts of mimicking the master's language transform the black into a source of threat: 'You had better keep your place' (*Black Skin*: 21). Mimicry also fails the colonized, even though in later commentators on Fanon, it serves as an act of resistance (Bhabha 2009b).

The intention behind mimic acts such as Amusa's or Perin Wadia's, to adapt Fanon's reading, is the quest for recognition: 'a world of reciprocal recognitions' (*Black Skin*: 170). The white master might grant the slave freedom (169), but this does not entail recognition. The slave does not secure – and here Fanon quotes Hegel – 'recognition as an independent self-consciousness' (170) thought. Thus, freedom *granted* rather than secured through struggle reinforces the black man's sense of non-selfhood. What Fanon proposes is that the black must secure his self-consciousness himself. This securing of self-consciousness, Fanon would argue, will be possible only within anti-colonial resistance, a theme to which we shall turn later. What is important, at this point, is to see Fanon's argument as a socio-psychological insight into colonialism:

- The black man loses all sense of the self because he is never acknowledged by the colonial master.
- In order to acquire this acknowledgment, the colonized starts wearing the white master's masks.

This wearing of masks in a quest for acknowledgement does not contribute to the acquisition of identity. It results, Fanon suggests, in neurosis, a schizophrenic condition of being split between black and white, and an inferiority complex born out of a conviction that his own culture is worthless and that the only culture worth possessing is that of the white man's. (This is akin to what W. E. B. DuBois, the early twentieth-century African American thinker, famously described as the black man's 'double consciousness' where the black man sees himself only through the white man's eyes. DuBois described the 'peculiar sensation … this sense of always looking at one's self through the eyes of. One ever feels his twoness, – an American, a Negro … two unreconciled strivings', 1961: 3. For a comparative study of the two thinkers, see Owens Moore 2005.)

THE BLACK MAN'S INFERIORITY COMPLEX AND RACE

Fanon argued that much of the black man's neurosis and inferiority complex and even aggression proceeded from the discovery that his colour represented evil, barbarism and depravity to the white colonial master. In Fanon's psychoanalysis of race, he suggests a social schema of black neurosis:

- The rejection of his culture by the colonizer results in a sense of loss in the colonized.
- The colonized internalizes this rejection of his culture, and begins to see his own culture as flawed, and is filled with shame and self-contempt.
- Myths of the white man's superiority and the black's inferiority are part of the socialization of the black from his very childhood.
- The black child (unlike the white child, for whom the family extends and fits into the social) sees a disconnect between his family and the larger social order, which is racist.
- Such a skewed socialization results in the black child seeking escape from his culture by incorporating cultural messages from white texts such as *Tarzan of the Apes*.
- Thus the child identifies himself with the white explorer in the stories, resulting in cultural trauma.

Fanon refers, in the very opening essay of *Black Skin*, to the western construction of the black man as a 'myth' – but a myth that the black has internalized so that he believes in it himself. As a result of this the black man does not want to behave like, or present himself as, a black man at all. He is expected to (by the white man) but is afraid of behaving 'like a nigger', as Fanon puts it (*Black Skin*: 86). This is the crisis of his social reality, his very existence, that the black man faces everyday. And because he feels he cannot ever be anything other than a black man, he begins to suffer a sense of worthlessness, inferiority and eventually slides into neurosis.

Fanon attributes a greater sensitivity to the black man as a result of this social reality of racism, or what he termed 'affective erethism' (*Black Skin*: 117–18). The hypersensitive black becomes extremely self-conscious of being black, suffering from 'shame' and 'self contempt' (88) in what he calls a 'situation neurosis' (43). His culture becomes a matter of shame, a burden and a mark of failure. Fanon's reading thus takes us from a social condition – racism – to its immediate consequence (an inferiority complex) and a far-reaching effect (neurosis). There is an additional causal factor in this neurosis, to which we now turn.

Treating North African immigrant workers, Fanon discovered that many suffered from alienation and 'affective erethism' because of the ruptured nature of the family. Fanon notes that all psychoanalytic theory and practice foregrounds the family. In the 'normal' course of events individuals discover a continuity of attitudes and belief systems between their immediate family and the larger social order and nation. There is no contradiction between what the individual sees and experiences within his family and the society in which his family lives. However, slavery and forced migration results in a massive rupture of this: the individual discovers that what he has seen/learnt in the (black) family clashes with the larger social order of *white* society. Fanon writes:

> A normal child that has grown up in a normal family will be a normal man. There is no disproportion between the life of the family and the life of the nation.
>
> (*Black Skin*: 110–11)

But for the European the family is aligned seamlessly with the nation and society. The family 'prefigures', as he puts it, a 'broader institution' (115).

As we can see Fanon is locating individual neurosis within the structure of the family as well as the society. For the white boy growing up into a white man in a white (or white-dominated society) stepping out of the family into the society does not constitute a radical rupture or shift. This is not the case with the black boy: 'A normal Negro child, having grown up within a normal family, will become abnormal on the slightest contact with the white world' (111).

The black boy growing up discovers that his family has little in common with the racist nation (what Fanon refers to as the 'disproportion between the life of the family and the life of the nation', *Black Skin:* 110). He faces contempt, rejection and amusement. His worth is not recognized, and he encounters the myth of black inferiority. Initiated into this myth the black man is confused: does his family not belong to the larger social order of the nation? Is the family an anomaly? Fanon argues that all Antilleans feel inferior and are neurotic – and this is not an individual trait but a social one. The 'taint', as he calls it, of neurosis comes from the environment – of colonialism

(*Black Skin*: 165). The problems of the black boys' psychopathology lay in the incongruity of the black family within the racialized white-dominated colonial system, not in the child or the family alone.

In order to alleviate this sense of shame, as we have already noted, the black man puts on a white mask. This serious game of putting on white masks begins with the socialization of the child itself, and Fanon spends some time painstakingly explaining the psychopathology engendered by this socialization in a racialized context.

Fanon argues that every society develops mechanisms for what he calls 'collective catharsis' (112), where there must exist an outlet through which the forces of rage and aggression must be released (112). The games children play, argues Fanon, are modes of such catharsis where excessive energies, frustrations and anger can be harmlessly expelled. Fanon lists the Tarzan stories, Mickey Mouse and adventure sagas as modes of 'collective catharsis'. Now this is where the colonial situation adds to the black child's burgeoning neurosis. The black child growing up in racialized, colonial situations has just 'discovered' the myth of African inferiority in these fantasmatic narratives. Tarzan becomes his hero, and the child begins identifying with the *white* explorers because even black children associate themselves, indeed identify themselves with the explorer, the white adventurer (113).

This fantastic narrative of violence and incorporation is the source of cultural trauma leading to neurosis for the black boy (Christian 2005: 222–3). The black child incorporates a fantasy which is at once misleadingly escapist and painful, traumatic and exhilarating. Later, grown up, the black man watching a movie with black villains is threatened by the 'negrophobic' gaze of the others around him as well as the sight of the black *imago* on the screen. The black man engages in a repetition of acts of spectatorship when he sees the screen: he recalls all the traumatic signifiers from the past, which have been put away but never erased.

During this process of assimilating new cultural messages that invoke older ones, of course, the black man also imbibes and assimilates the prejudices and ideological doctrines embedded in these stories. Since he has already encountered the myth of the evil black man, these stories reinforce within him the myth of white superiority in a 'crystallization' of an attitude and a 'way of thinking and seeing' (114). Frustrated and confused, he seeks modes of resolving the identity crisis. The black boy also adopts these same Eurocentric, racist and colonial stories for himself. The white mask has just been slipped on – a process of whitening or 'lactification' (Fanon's term, *Black Skin:* 33) – and the black boy's journey into slavery, objectification and neurosis has begun. Ironically, the white mask is what highlights the blackness beneath: *he will always be a black man wearing a white mask.* Fanon frames this complex in the form of a famous question-and-answer binary: 'What does the black man want? ... The black man wants to be white' (*Black Skin*: 1, 3). It is in the attempt to acquire recognition from the whites that the blacks reinforce their inferiority complex.

Fanon has proved here that the inferiority complex in the black man is clearly historical and social. And it is through this historical and social grounding that he would critique one of the most influential psychoanalytic interpretations of the colonial condition: Octave Mannoni's famous theory of the black man's 'dependency complex'.

THE DEPENDENCY COMPLEX

Fanon's reading of the colonial situation was a response to Octave Mannoni's work on the 'psychology of colonialism' in his work, *Prospero and Caliban: The Psychology of Colonization* (1950, English trans., 1964). Mannoni argued that the African suffered from an 'inferiority complex' that was further aggravated by the colonial situation. He proposed 'archetypes' of the colonizer and colonized personalities: the colonizer was prone to be in control and dominate, while the African sought dependency. In the colonial context these personalities receive nourishment. Mannoni also argued that the white master is seen as a father-substitute. Unwilling to be without a protector, the black man seeks/ sees the paternal role in the European. When the native believes, rightly or wrongly, that he is being abandoned by his paternalistic European master, his dependence causes him to rebel. Mannoni (infamously) explained (away) the 1947 rebellion and massacres (one hundred thousand Malagasies killed by French troops) as the result of this feeling of abandonment. Colonial policies, he argued, the hardships of the Second World War and other circumstances resulted in what he identified as a child-like rage in the colonized. The colonial masters, instead of recognizing this sentiment, reacted brutally. Mannoni therefore was treating the role of brutal colonial authority and feelings of nationalism (among the Malagasies) as incidental to the horrific events, attributing everything to the 'dependency complex' of the colonized.

> Mannoni argued that the whites and blacks had specific psychic states: the white man was prone to dominate while the black man was prone to be dominated. Mannoni suggested that the colonial situation enabled both these 'roles' to be played out in the racial encounter where the white man consistently dominates the black man.

Fanon begins his refutation of Mannoni's psychologizing by first offering a socio-economic analysis of a colonial condition. He defines South Africa as 'a boiler into which thirteen million blacks are clubbed and penned in by two and a half million whites' (*Black Skin*: 64). The inferiority complex of the black man is undeniable, says Fanon, but it proceeds from colonialism's social and economic realities (4). He underscores the material-economic basis of racism and argues that fears and desires – psychological states – arise out of these conditions. Mannoni claimed that any member of a minority race/group in a group of a different colour would feel threatened. Fanon rejects this outright, noting that in Martinique there are two hundred whites who dominate three hundred thousand people of colour, while in South Africa there are two million whites against almost thirteen million native people. In neither of these societies has a black felt he was superior to the (minority) whites (68).

Take a literary text as an instance here of the ways in which colonialism enables the numerically minoritarian whites to lord it over the numerically superior Asians: the English novelist Rudyard Kipling (1865–1936) and his classic work, *Kim* (1901). The novel opens with young Kim kicking the native boys off a cannon, in a powerful metaphor of white domination. Later, Kipling shows how a venerable Asian lama becomes emotionally and even physically dependent upon the young Irish boy in the colonial context. It is the callow youth, by virtue of his racial identity and his location (the British Empire), who is able to lead the Asians. In the colonial context, Kipling suggests a dependency based on racial identities alone: the white boy, despite his age, will always lead and the Asian subjects will always be led.

Mannoni went on to claim that the only means for the black man of erasing, or at least suppressing, his 'inferiority complex' is to generate a relationship of dependency on the European. Fanon disputes this by proposing that the black man's feelings of inferiority are not, as

Mannoni seems to think, 'natural'. Inferiority is not a natural psychological state but one that results from colonialism's socialization, material states and indoctrination. Fanon proposes that the black feels inferior because the white projects himself as superior: '*It is the racist who creates his inferior*' (*Black Skin*: 69, emphasis in original). What Fanon is suggesting is that Mannoni's analysis *presupposes* particular complexes when, in reality, it is the colonial situation that enables the construction and rise of these complexes. The sheer brutality facilitated by colonialism enables the European to feel superior and the concomitant feelings of inferiority of the colonized (74).

Mannoni famously proposed that the rifle in the hands of the European becomes a phallic symbol. Fanon dismisses such psychoanalytic interpretations that reduce material conditions to symbolic representations in one sentence: 'The rifle [in the dream of a Malagasy man] is not a penis but a genuine rifle, model Lebel 1916' (*Black Skin*: 79). The fear of the rifle, and the colonial apparatus, is not just of the *symbol* of the rifle but the fear of what it can really do to flesh, blood and bones.

Fanon's critique here foregrounds the concrete socio-economic conditions in which particular personalities, neuroses and psychopathological disorders emerge. For such race-induced neurosis, Fanon would then argue, colonial psychiatric medicine had no real solutions – because this medicine itself emerged from a colonial context.

'MENTAL DISORDERS' AND COLONIAL PSYCHIATRY

Jimmie, the eponymous hero of Australian novelist Thomas Keneally's *The Chant of Jimmie Blacksmith* (1973), sets out on a spree of murders. The description of the moments before he takes up the axe and sets out to hack four white women to death goes thus:

> He was in a fever for some definite release … Jimmie admitted to his body's judgmental majesty, a sense that the sharp-edged stars impelled him. He felt large with a royal fever, with re-birth …
>
> (Keneally, 1973: 78)

The sense of bottled anger, the feverish madness of this wronged and unfairly treated 'half-breed' (Jimmie is the son of an Aboriginal woman and an itinerant white missionary) illustrates Fanon's theory that the colonized's violence and madness are the products of the colonial system, and not immanent to the African or Asian.

In his second thesis of the opening essay on the 'North African syndrome' in *Toward the African Revolution,* Fanon writes: 'the North African does not come with a substratum common to his race, but on a foundation built by the European' (7). Fanon suggests that every North African who visits the doctor 'bears the dead weight of all his compatriots' (8). He is treated as 'undisciplined', inconsequential and insincere (10). Fanon pleads for a 'situational diagnosis' that recognizes the cultural contexts of specific illnesses, proposing that the black is in a 'perpetual state of insecurity'. He does not fit into his social circles, into his workplace or his community – and all these contribute to his neurosis (12–13).

What Fanon is suggesting is a critique of colonial medicine and psychiatric practices, where individual psychosis and the prevailing colonial political conditions are linked (Vergès 1996: 49). The North African's ailments and pains are not treated as authentic by the European doctors, who function from within a European framework into which the African is forced. Fanon proposes that the African ailments must be linked to the man's social life: the African has no friends, his only preoccupation is labour, and his sexual contacts are restricted to prostitutes (*African*: 11). His social setting induces sickness, argues Fanon. Thus psychoanalysis, rooted in an anti-black, pro-white context (as an early commentator on Fanon's use of psychoanalysis summarizes it: see Butts 1979) was of little help in psychiatry because its very frames of interpretation marginalized the language, symptoms and neurosis of the African, even as these frames – of colonial domination – induced neurosis.

When the patient enters the hospital, he is unable to formulate his symptoms.

> He [the African] tells about his pain … he now talks about it volubly … He takes it, touches it with his ten fingers, develops it, exposes it. It grows as one watches it. He gestures it over the whole surface of his body and after fifteen minutes of gestured explanations the interpreter (appropriately baffling) translates for us: he says he has a belly-ache.
>
> (*African*: 5)

Fanon reports an intern complaining: 'I can't help it, I can't talk to them in the same way that I talk to other patients' (*African*: 9). Fanon's examples are a critique of colonial institutional, epistemic as well as narrative – the way the patient is expected to *tell* his story – frames that presuppose symptoms, etiology and cure.

Fanon, as noted above, was interested in social psychology, in the historical and social conditions that induce sickness. In his other work on psychological disorders and psychiatric testing, Fanon argued that tests such as TAT were created with the western mind as the object of study. The African subject of these tests was often perplexed and therefore failed them. This, for Fanon, was the result of the cultural bias of psychological testing (he, in fact, developed a test specifically for the Maghreb: see Bullard 2005).

Fanon's last chapter in *Wretched* was on 'colonial war and mental disorders'. Here he reiterates his argument that the violence in the Algerian is because of the social and economic contexts he finds himself in, and over which he has no control. 'Colonization, in its very essence', writes Fanon, 'already appeared to be a great purveyor of psychiatric hospitals' (*Wretched*: 181). The case studies of reactionary psychosis Fanon lists in this chapter function as evidence that the colonial war, with its bombings, arrests and tortures, is the causal factor in mental illnesses among the Algerians. Other mental illnesses among children, suicidal tendencies and ulcers are psychosomatic, in Fanon's reading. Rigid muscles and facial freezing are conditions that seem peculiar to Algerian men, notes Fanon. This is how Fanon interprets the disorder: '[it is] simply a postural concurrence and evidence in the colonized's muscles of their rigidity, their reticence and refusal in the face of the colonial authorities' (217).

Fanon then turns to standard European psychiatric evaluations of the Algerian mind/personality: that the Algerian is a habitual killer, that he is a savage, senseless killer, and that robbery by an Algerian involves breaking and entering but also murder (222–3). Fanon focuses on this theme of Algerian criminality in some detail, addressing various physicians and theorists as he goes along. He calls into question the theory (myth) that the 'criminal impulsiveness of the North African is the transcription of a certain configuration of the nervous system into his pattern of behavior' (227–8). 'The idleness of the frontal lobes explains his indolence, his crimes, his thefts, his rapes, and his lies', writes Fanon (228). Hence the colonial psychiatric fraternity seeks to 'discipline, tame, subdue … and … pacify' – words, Fanon notes, that are common to colonialists in the occupied territories (228).

Fanon argues that the psychiatric assessment of the Algerian as criminal is accepted and assimilated as correct (229). Frustrated by his inability to attack his true enemy, the white man, the Algerian turns against his own kind. It is the high-pressure *environment* of colonialism that makes the Algerian take the knife to another Algerian. Having been 'exposed to daily incitement to murder' from his poverty, the sight of his starving family, unemployment and exploitation, the colonial subject is filled with hatred, even towards his fellow countrymen whom he sees as rivals (231). This hatred manifests as explosive violence, some of which is directed against his own fellowmen. The violence in the colonial, amongst the colonized, is therefore a mode of release: when the colonized are unable to kill the white master, their rage mounts and turns against their countrymen.

But, notes Fanon, criminality among Algerians was diminishing since the war began, for the simple reason that the colonial situation that drove the black to violence had altered to a state of war (230). If the colonials were correct in their belief about the 'natural' and innate savagery of the Africans, then there is no possible reason for this change. However, Fanon had an explanation for the change in the Algerian's personality. He asks: 'Could it be said that the war, the privileged terrain for expressing finally a collective aggressiveness, directs congenitally murderous acts at the occupier?' (230). Finally, the colonized is able to *legitimately* fuel his rage, and direct it against what Fanon calls the 'national enemy' (231). Fanon proposes that the national struggle has 'channeled' the black's anger (230). Given the opportunity to harness his frustrations and rage into a coherent action plan directed at the annihilation of his perpetual enemy, the colonizer, the Algerian begins to shed his 'criminality' towards his fellow countrymen.

Thus Fanon locates the violent personality, the mental illness and the possible cure within the colonial system. His 'sociogenic' interpretation refuses biological and genetic determinism in order to demonstrate the frightening effects of colonial domination. What is significant in Fanon's reading is that the medical, psychiatric and epistemological violence of the colonial regime leaves very little of the colonized's life untouched.

SUMMARY

Fanon's psychoanalysis of the colonial situation achieves a major shift: from individual psycho-pathological states to social contexts and sources (aetiology) of neurosis.

He begins by proposing that all identity is relational, where the Self can understand its identity only in relation to the Other, or another. In the colonial context the black man only sees himself as the negative of the white man, where white is the norm, and black the deviation from the norm. The black man only sees himself as an object, with no sense of the Self because the white only sees him as an object. There is no self-recognition, no self-awareness in the black man in the colonial situation. In order to escape from the condition of being mere object, the black man seeks to *become* white: he craves recognition from the white man. In order to acquire this acknowledgment, the colonized starts wearing the white master's masks.

The black man's feelings of inferiority are not, Fanon argues, 'natural'. Inferiority in the black results from colonialism's socialization, material conditions (exploitation, oppression, violence) and indoctrination. Fanon further proposes that the black feels inferior because the white projects himself as superior.

Fanon thus engages in a 'situational diagnosis' that recognizes the cultural contexts of specific illnesses among blacks. Colonial medicine and psychiatric practices fail to recognize the social contexts of black neurosis because these practices emerge from the same European paradigm.

One of the features we have noted thus far is Fanon's emphasis on the black *man* within the colonial situation. In later essays Fanon also turned his attention to the woman question in colonialism, a topic that has elicited numerous and frequently furious debates about his gender politics. It is to the gender reading within Fanon's works that the next chapter addresses itself.

4

COLONIALISM, GENDER AND SEXUALITY

In Chicano/a activist and playwright Cherríe Moraga's (b. 1952) *The Hungry Woman* (2001), a futuristic play about the Chicano/a 'nation' of Aztlán, Moraga's characters Savannah and Mama Sal exchange this dialogue:

MAMA-SAL: We were content to for awhile –

SAVANNAH: Sort of. Until the revolutionaries told the women, put down your guns and pick up your babies … And into the kitchen!

(Moraga 2001: 21)

Leila, who eventually descends into madness in Assia Djebar's *Women of Algiers in their Apartment* (1999), calls out to her 'sisters':

Where are you, you fire carriers, you my sisters, who should have liberated the city … Barbed wire no longer obstructs the alleys, now it decorates windows, balconies, anything at all that opens onto an outside space.

(Djebar 1999: 44)

The 'fire carriers' are now a source of threat. During the revolution the women abandoned traditional roles and picked up guns, went into public places, fought alongside the men but the moment the nation is liberated the women are forced to return to the circumscribed space of hearth and home, and become good wives and mothers. Moraga's and Djebar's accounts here capture many of the gender-sexuality themes that concerned Fanon in his discussion of militancy, nationalism and anti-colonial struggles.

Fanon's analysis of the colonial situation and its effects on black subjectivity takes the black *man* as the norm. Despite this emphasis on male subjectivity Fanon's work also exhibits a continued concern with the sexualized nature of colonial domination – and this concern is the subject of the present chapter.

Fanon's exploration of colonialism's sexual dimensions and gendered nature could be studied under the following heads:

- colonialism and its sexual economy;
- colonialism and gender-sexual violence;
- women, the anti-colonial struggle and the veil.

COLONIALISM AND ITS SEXUAL ECONOMY

Fanon sees the sexual economy as intrinsic to the colonial condition. This sexual economy is visible in at least four forms:

- The woman circulates as a token of exchange between the black man and the white.
- Europeans imagine/perceive the black woman as an exotic–erotic object.
- The Algerian woman's veil thwarts this colonizing gaze of desire, and the colonizer therefore resents it.
- Colonialism's attempts to 'unveil' the Algerian woman are symptomatic of the desire to 'penetrate' Algeria itself.

Sexual economy is a shorthand term to describe the ways in which sex and sexual identity enable social relations. For instance, the use of women to sell products, their use as low-paid workers, the depiction of women as repositories of tradition by fundamentalists or moralists in order to speak of the crisis in a culture, the exchange of women to seal connections between communities or families, the emphasis in the woman's reproductive abilities, the restrictions on women's sexuality, the money made out of pornography (which portrays women as sex objects) all constitute the sexual economy.

The first moments of the crisis of the colonized man's subjectivity occurs when the black man recognizes the *gaze* of the white man: 'look, a negro' (*Black Skin*: 84). It is the visual perception that produces *racial difference*. The black man, when he hears the white child's comment ('Look, a negro ... Mum, look a negro') and sees himself through the white man's gaze, begins to perceive a lack in himself. The loss of self-hood in the black man originates first in the visual field of colonialism. Fanon mourns the colonized condition of the black where he becomes self-conscious of being black: even when watching a film, writes Fanon, the black man believes the people are 'watching ... examining ... waiting' for him (*Black Skin:* 108). Fanon shows how the black man's subjectivity and sense of self emerges in this context of racial difference, articulated within the visual regime of white spectactorship. This visual regime is also structured around a sexual economy, specifically the woman.

Women in Fanon are mostly the objects of male/masculine desire, and he has little interest in feminine desire, as emblematized in his question (which in itself, ironically, recalls, Freud's 'what does the woman want?'): what does the black man want? (*Black Skin:* 1). In his essay 'Algeria Unveiled' (*Dying*) Fanon turned to the 'woman's question'. He begins with the European imagining of the black woman as an exotic object:

A strand of hair, a bit of forehead, a segment of an 'overwhelmingly beautiful face' glimpsed in a streetcar or on a train, may suffice to keep alive and strengthen the European's persistence in his irrational conviction that the Algerian woman is the queen of all women.

(*Dying*: 43)

Fanon suggests a racialized visual regime of colonialism here where the Algerian woman is the *object* of the white man's desire.

The veil thwarts this colonizing gaze of desire, and the colonizer therefore resents it because, as Fanon puts it 'she [the Algerian woman] does not yield herself' (*Dying*: 44). The veil functions as the object of unruly desire and control, of fear and fetish. Her unveiling therefore becomes central to the colonial pathology of control: 'Unveiling this woman is revealing her beauty; it is baring her secret, breaking her resistance, making her available for adventure' (43). What is interesting is Fanon's interpretation of the veil as a symbol of colonial homogenization: regional variants of the men's veil exist, but in the case of the woman's veil, it 'is a uniform which tolerates no modification, no variant' (36). Fanon draws attention here, albeit indirectly, to two structural conditions: *patriarchy and colonialism*, where the non-white woman is subject to a particular set of standards and regimentation.

It is obvious that Fanon sees the colonial visual regime as mapping the woman onto Algeria and vice versa before seeking control over both. Colonial rulings and attempts to 'unveil' the woman become symptomatic, Fanon argues, of the 'penetration' (8, 42) the colonial male seeks into the society and culture of the colonized. The 'bared faces and freed bodies' mark the (desired) shift of the colonized woman into the culture of the colonizer, a process Fanon terms 'conversion' (42, 43). Fanon writes: the 'rape of the Algerian woman in the dream of a European is always preceded by a rending of the veil' (45). What Fanon refers to as 'double deflowering' is a process where sexuality and race come together to dominate the Algerian woman. Subsequently, Fanon positions the veiled woman of Algeria as both a symbol and embodied reality of Algeria's anti-colonial struggles. The veiled woman holds great significance for Fanon. He sees her as embodying the revolutionary spirit of Algeria (66), even though he is not really interested in her subjectivity (Bergner 1995: 85).

This western interest in the 'problem' of the veiled Arab woman has not altogether disappeared. In fact, Fanon's insights into the power game implicit in the veiling/unveiling metaphor remain relevant even today, given the fact that the rescue of the oppressed Muslim woman has been central, and even 'amplified' in the rhetoric of the early twenty-first century's 'war on terror' (Wallach Scott 2007; Gilroy 2010: 19).

Fanon argues that the black man also sees the white woman as a means of reestablishing his masculinity – which, as we have seen, has been destroyed by the colonial apparatus when he is reduced to just a black body. Thus the black man, in Fanon's reading, simply wishes to 'go to bed with a white woman'. The desire, writes Fanon, marks a 'wish to be white. A lust for revenge, in any case' (*Dying*: 6). The white men, in turn, are perpetually worried that their women are at the mercy of the blacks (122).

What is clear from this argument is that the woman circulates as a token of exchange between the black man and the white:

- The white man fears the rape of the white woman by the black man.

- The white man wishes to tear the veil and possess the Algerian woman and thus symbolically possess Algeria itself.
- The black man wishes for nothing more than sex with the white woman as a revenge for his own emasculation at the hands of the white male master.

What Fanon clearly emphasizes is not only the sexual economy of colonialism, but also the potential for violence inherent within this economy, and it is to this theme of sexual- and gender-related violence I now turn.

COLONIALISM AND SEXUAL VIOLENCE

Ronald Merrick, the policeman in Paul Scott's empire saga, *The Raj Quartet*, is offended by the Indian Hari Kumar because Kumar has better accented English and clearly belongs to a higher class, despite being of the subject race (Kumar calls himself Harry Coomer). When Kumar is arrested, it is Merrick who interrogates him and, during the process, sexually abuses him as well. Racial dominance here folds into sexual violence. Merrick's sexuality finds its most violent expression when he has a brown man as his captive. In parallel, his racism finds expression in the form of sexual abuse. In the colony, Scott suggests, sexual violence against the colonized male can come from the white homosexual who is able to use his racialized role as ruler to dominate him.

In Thomas Keneally's *The Chant of Jimmie Blacksmith* the landowner Healy is abusive towards Jimmie, the servant, when the latter asks for a letter of reference. Eventually, Jimmie realizes that Healy's annoyance with him is because he, Healy, cannot write (23). The white man exhibits his inadequacy in the presence of his black servant. In Scott's work, Kumar/Coomer is obviously the better educated of the two – and it is this class difference that Merrick resents. Despite his superior social status, Kumar/Coomer is reduced to an ordinary prisoner because the racial difference empowers the white Merrick. Merrick's unreasonable hatred of Kumar/Coomer also finds its origins in the deracination of the Indian. As Kumar/Coomer appears whiter than Merrick himself, Merrick uses sexual violence and abuse as a means of reinstating what he presumes is his racial superiority.

When the white man's social inadequacy is revealed in the encounter with the black, it provokes the white man to the abuse of the black/brown male. This abuse is possible because, in the racialized colonial context, the native has little or no power. The native male becomes the subject of violence that is sexualized in the case of Kumar/Coomer.

Fanon argues that:

- sexual perversities (under which he includes homosexuality) and violence are intrinsic to the colonial condition;
- sexual hierarchies cannot be delinked from the racial hierarchies which enable an acting-out of perversities.

Sexual violence, in Fanon's reading, is common to both, white and black, men and women, due to the very nature of their racial interactions. The white man seeks to overcome his inferiority (both Merrick and Healy recognize their inferiority in comparison with their black/ brown subjects) through violence targeted at the black/brown man.

In Fanon's analysis of colonial psychopathology the black man is a 'phobogenic object' (*Black Skin*: 117). The subject of white fantasies, the black man functions primarily (only?) as a sexual threat: 'A Negro is raping me'. Fanon reads this as the white woman's fantasy of having sex with the black man, lesbianism, a wish for self-mutilation and even narcissism. Fanon writes: 'when a woman lives the fantasy of rape by a Negro, it is in some way the fulfillment of a private dream, of an inner wish. [I]t is the woman who rapes herself' (138). In similar fashion, the European's view of the Muslim man as inherently violent – of 'the connections between the Muslim psyche and blood' – expresses a certain fascination for the same (*Wretched*: 222; for feminist criticism of Fanon's argument see Doane 1991; Brownmiller 1975).

Rape and sexual relations of/with the black woman by the white man were accepted as routine modes of retaining colonial dominance (Woodhull cited in Faulkner 1996). Fanon's reading of the white woman's so-called fantasy of rape at the hands of the black man is itself the result of the perversity of colonial relations. In other words, if the now-neurotic black man seeks vengeance through the (fantasized or real) rape of the white woman, the white woman develops her own neurosis about her (desired?) rape at the hands of the black man (Sharpley-Whiting 1998).

As Scott's and Keneally's tales suggest, colonial violence often takes the form of sexual violence (Jimmie finally kills all the women in the novel). Sexual violence as perversion is thus conflated with issues of class, racial superiority, colonialism and colonial law. The white man remains in an empowered position over the colonized despite serious failings, such as illiteracy, because the colonial condition *allows* unequal social relations.

Fanon argues that the colonizer's hatred for the black man is a symptom of his sexual perversity. Black and gay, in Fanon, are mutually exclusive because he sees homosexuality as the domain of the racist white man, and as a debilitating condition (Mercer 1999; also Dollimore 1991; Fuss 1994; Goldie 1999. For more sympathetic readings of Fanon's 'homophobia' see Seshadri-Crooks 2002; James 1997; Dubey 1998). Just as the white woman both fears and desires the black man, the 'Negrophobic man is a repressed homosexual' (*Black Skin:* 121). Fanon devotes considerable space to the question of sexual perversion, which he aligns (problematically) with homosexuality. Here he sees the cornerstone of the pathology of colonialism: racism and homosexuality combined in the white man. He speaks, therefore, of 'hate complexes' whose components include 'fault, guilt, refusal of guilt, paranoia – one is back in homosexual territory' (*Black Skin*: 141).

Fanon also argues that the white man's sexual perversity, complexes and brutality are the result of his history: the white man is aware that one of his ancestors has killed another man. In the colonies, fearing reprisals, the white man reproduces the violence of his ancestors and therefore installs the master–slave relationship with the black man.

The violent fantasies of rape and penetration, however, also result in a different theme in colonialism. Fanon now turns to the veiled Algerian woman not merely as the imminent target of the white man's violent sexual fantasies but also as a possible weapon in the anti-colonial struggle.

WOMEN, THE ANTI-COLONIAL STRUGGLE AND THE VEIL

In Assia Djebar's *Women of Algiers in their Apartment*, a text we have already cited, the woman in Algeria would feel threatened, and would be perceived as *threatening*:

> Yesterday, the master made his authority felt in the closed, feminine spaces through the single presence of his gaze alone, annihilating those of other people. In turn, the feminine eye when it moves around is now, it seems, *feared*

> *by the men* immobilized in the Moorish cafes of today's medinas, while the
> white phantom, unreal but enigmatic, passes through.
>
> (Djebar 1999; 138, emphasis added)

In sharp contrast to the image of the veiled woman as erotic object,
Djebar proposes the veiled woman as a threat here.

Thus far we have seen how the veiled Algerian woman is the object
of the white man's desire, and so the focus of colonialism's oppression.
Fanon, however, also sees the veiled woman as connected to the anti-
colonial struggle. He treats the veil as embodying specific values within
the colonial encounter:

- It serves as a *threat* to the colonizer because he cannot penetrate
  the guise.
- It becomes a *weapon* when the Algerian woman re-asserts her right
  to veil herself, but also uses it as a disguise.

The Algerian anti-colonial struggle itself can be examined through
the stages that the adoption and abandonment of the veil goes
through, according to Fanon. In the first stage, when faced with the
colonizer's brutal laws, the veil is more tightly wound. There is a 'cult
of the veil'. In the second stage, when the Algerian woman also joins the
anti-colonial struggle (with some anxiety and resistance on the part of
the Algerian *men* whose attitude to the arming of their women, and their
participation in public life is, at best, ambivalent), she converts the veil
into 'revolutionary fashion', suggesting that she enjoys a certain agency
in the choice of being veiled or not. Yet Fanon understands that in
underdeveloped countries feudal conditions might prevent the women
from becoming a part of the political movement. Fanon warns that
in such conditions care must be taken 'not to perpetuate feudal traditions
that give priority to men over women'. Women must be given equal
importance to men not merely in token political representation but
what Fanon calls 'daily life': schools and assemblies (*Wretched*: 141–2).

As the woman does diverse and more dangerous work for the liberation movement, she begins to alter gender-specific roles as well. Fanon
casts the actions of the woman in the second stage of the revolution in
consciously psychoanalytic terms: the 'Algerian woman penetrates into
the flesh of the Revolution' (*Dying*: 54). The veil is no more a sign of
passive acquiescence or fetish object. Instead, it has become a sign of

power. Despite being veiled, Fanon suggests, she has acquired power and destabilized gender as well as racist power relations. In the third stage, the woman becomes what Fanon calls a 'woman-arsenal'. Fanon describes the woman soldier in glowing terms:

> Carrying revolvers, grenades, hundreds of false identity cards or bombs, the unveiled Algerian woman moves like a fish in the Western waters. The soldiers, the French patrols, smile to her as she passes, compliments on her good looks are heard here and there, but no one suspects that her suitcases contain the automatic pistol which will presently mow down four or five members of one of the patrols.
>
> (*Dying*: 58)

'Traditional' femininity is subverted in this stage. The veil reappears, but for devastating (militant) reasons: she seeks to conceal her identity before unleashing the power of arms she carries with her. Fanon writes of the woman who seeks to 'conceal the package from the eyes of the occupier and again to cover [her]self with the protective *haik*' (*Dying*: 61). Concealment here is a strategy: 'Showing empty and apparently mobile and free hands is the sign that disarms the enemy soldier' (62). In what is an extraordinary reading, Fanon proposes that in the third stage the woman adds layers to herself, appears fuller and padded, 'shapeless' as Fanon calls it so that she can conceal and carry weaponry, thus marking a shift from the second stage where she appeared thin and minimized (62). The veil, in Fanon's reading, gains a new value in the anti-colonial struggle. Incidentally, here a particular cultural practice serves as an anti-colonial device (Yeğenoğlu 1998: 64; for feminist critiques of this argument, see Mernissi 1987; Hatem 1993; Mama 1995; Fuss 1994; Chow 1999. Support for Fanon's 'pro-feminist' stance has emerged in African American theorist bell hooks 1996 and Sharpley-Whiting 1998. Homi Bhabha argues that in Fanon 'man' is taken to 'connote … a phenomenological quality of humanness, inclusive of man and woman', 2008: xxxvi–xxxvii).

The veil therefore now appears as a weapon itself, a mimicry (a conscious act, as opposed to masquerade, which is an unconscious assumption of a role) that helps the woman 'penetrate' the colonizer's camp. She assumes camouflage, carrying heavy weaponry under her veil and native costume but all the while pretending she is carrying nothing. Fanon goes on to argue that the Algerian woman thus reinvents herself, that she fits into European modernity, but remains an 'authentic birth in a true state' (*Dying*: 50). Such a reinvention of the woman is crucial to the nation's reinvention itself, suggests Fanon: 'the freedom of the Algerian people from then on became identified with woman's liberation, with her entry into history' (107). Fanon warns that in the post-independence state, the formerly colonized must guard against perpetuating feudal structures that oppress the woman and valorize the masculine. He cautions the formerly colonized against returning to pre-colonial fascisms and patriarchy (Haddour 2010). This is a crucial argument – for here we can see signs of Fanon's pro-feminist position.

We see this anxiety over the masculine, patriarchal version of nationalism in several texts. Beatrice in Nigerian novelist Chinua Achebe's (b. 1930) *Anthills of the Savannah* tells Chris in a tone marked by both fury and sorrow, 'the story of this country, as far as you are concerned, is the story of the three of you [men]' (1988: 66). Here Beatrice indicts the close linkage of nationalism, anti-colonial struggles and unfortunate patriarchy. This alignment, in Fanon's view, must change.

Fanon here treats the veil as marking:

- the reinvention of the Algerian woman as a revolutionary (Cornell 2001; Dubey 1998);
- the retrieval of cultural symbols for anti-colonial purposes.

Once the woman strategically accepts the veil (or the gun), it can no longer function as a symbol of patriarchal control, or the 'natural' feminine. That is, the act of taking up the gun or putting on the veil is treated as an act of feminine *agency* in Fanon's analysis (for counter arguments about the role of the veiled Algerian woman as revolutionary and the agency of the woman, see Macey 2000: 403; Helie-Lucas 1990; McClintock 1999. McClintock elsewhere suggests that Fanon's reading assumes a certain 'semiotic innocence' of the veil as object, and ignores the restrictive Islamic pre-colonial conditions the veil helped impose on the woman, 1995: 365).

SUMMARY

Fanon was deeply interested in the gender and sexual dimensions of colonial domination. All colonial domination, his work shows, depends on *both* racial and sexual hierarchies, and both these hierarchies carry the potential for violence.

The Algerian woman, in this colonial sexual economy, circulates as a token of exchange between the black man and the white. She becomes the erotic object of the European's perception and imagination. But because she is veiled, she becomes an impenetrable object. Fanon argues that the white colonial's attempts to 'unveil' the Algerian woman represent his desire to 'penetrate' Algeria itself. Here the woman functions as a symbol of an entire nation and culture.

On the obverse side of this sexual economy is the white woman. Fanon proposes that the black man begins to see the white woman as a means of re-establishing his masculinity, which colonialism has destroyed. He therefore fantasizes about raping the white woman as a revenge for his own emasculation at the hands of the white male master.

Such fantasies are essentially violent. Fanon argues that sexual perversity and violence are intrinsic to the colonial condition because sexual hierarchies cannot be delinked from racial hierarchies.

Fanon then proceeds to examine the role of the veiled woman within the anti-colonial struggle. As the woman begins to undertake more dangerous work for the liberation movement, she begins to alter pre-assigned gender-specific roles. She now seeks to conceal her identity under the veil before unleashing the power of arms she carries with her. She thus converts her native costume into camouflage. This, Fanon argues, is the reinvention of the Algerian woman. Such a reinvention of the woman is crucial to the nation's reinvention itself, suggests Fanon.

Fanon thus takes the nature of colonial violence and addresses it from its sexual-gender angle. However, this is only one component of his extended discussion of violence, a discussion that is perhaps the most recognized within Fanon's oeuvre.

5

ON VIOLENCE I

The Destruction of the Self

In Pakistani author Bapsi Sidhwa's (b. 1938) *Cracking India* (originally published as *Ice-candy man*, 1991), a novel about the Indian Partition of 1947, friends turn bitter enemies when the British leave the subcontinent. The novel maps the slow descent into chaos of Indian and Muslim populations massacring each other as the British, having done the damage by 'constructing' the spectre of communalism, abandon their former subjects. Nigerian-British author Buchi Emecheta's (b. 1944) novel *Destination Biafra* (1982) deals with the Nigerian civil war in which cruelties were perpetrated by the formerly colonized on each other. In all of Chinua Achebe's fiction we see the alienation of the individual as well as a culture/society due to the impact of a brutal colonial regime. In Australian Thomas Keneally's novel, *The Chant of Jimmie Blacksmith,* to which I have already referred, the 'half-breed' Jimmie, whose soul seems lost under the oppression and injustices of colonialism, explodes into inexplicable violence. The acts of barbaric killing are, Jimmy understands, inhuman. Yet his rage as an exploited native under the whites demands this inhuman gratification so that he can develop a sense of the self. Each of these novels suggests that postcolonial violence is a legacy of colonialism: whether in the form of communalism, economic exploitation or the creation of a bourgeois class that inherits the mantle of its former colonial master.

When Fanon opened his *Wretched* with a chapter on violence, he ensured that it would remain the one theme consistently associated with his thought. Fanon has been seen as an apostle of violence. Several thinkers (Arendt 1970; Taylor 1994: 65; Bulhan 1985: 137–53; Nandy 1992: 33–4; Serequeberhan 1994) since then have grappled with what looks like an advocacy of violence on the one hand and a deeply humanist thought on the other in Fanon's writings.

There are two kinds of violence in Fanon.

The first is colonial violence, or the *violence of the colonizer*. This violence results in an annihilation of (i) the body of the colonized, (ii) the psyche of the colonized and (iii) the culture of the colonized. This kind of violence is rooted in the very structure of colonialism and occurs across multiple domains: economic, cultural, psychological, physical and spatial.

Fanon proposes that it is colonial violence and its trauma that leads to the second form of violence – that from the colonized's side.

The second is the *violence of the colonized*. This violence is an attempt on the part of the desperate, frustrated and alienated colonized subject to retrieve a certain dignity and sense of the Self that colonial violence had destroyed. It takes the form of anti-colonial struggles.

This chapter deals with colonial violence ('Violence I'), and the subsequent chapter with the colonized's violence ('Violence II').

COLONIAL VIOLENCE

In Chinua Achebe's *Arrow of God* Winterbottom, the District Officer, proudly tells his subordinate:

> I think I can say with all modesty that this change came after I had gathered and publicly destroyed all firearms, except of course, this collection here. You will be going there frequently on tour. If you hear anyone talking about Otiji-Egbe, you know that they are talking about me. Otiji-Egbe means "Breaker of Guns." I am even told that all children born in that year belong to a new age-grade of the Breaking of the Guns.

(Achebe 1977: 37)

The violence of the officer's act has entered into the cultural memory of the colonized. It is not possible to distinguish, Achebe suggests, which is the greater violence – the brutality of the oppressor, or the traumatic recall of the events in the very idiom and speech of the colonized.

Ghanaian playwright Ama Ata Aidoo (b. 1942) in her play *Anowa* (1970) makes the suggestion that the protagonist Kofi Aiko's impotence might be the result of imperial domination. His emasculation becomes a symbol of the erosion of the sense of the Self under colonialism. Even the histories of the colonial 'discovery' of African, Australian or South American cultures are histories of this white-violence-cast-as-discovery. Australian Aboriginal author Mudrooroo (b. 1938) writes of Australian, Maori and New Zealand history:

> All New Zealand schoolchildren were taught about Captain James Cook's discovery of New Zealand and his historic landfall ... But what the schoolchildren are not told is that Cook's first landing was marked by the killing of a Maori called Te Maro, shot through the heart by a musket bullet.
>
> (quoted in Crane 2001: 395)

Each of these texts emphasizes the cultural violence of colonialism, whether in their histories of the African or Asian nations, their evangelicalism or their civilizational mission. Colonialism's cultural mission, Achebe, Aidoo and Mudrooroo suggest, results in the erasure of local/native cultures. This erasure is clearly an act of violence, for it alienates the colonized from their traditions, histories and cultures.

Fanon's key arguments about the various forms of colonial violence may be summarized as follows:

- Colonialism was inherently a violent phenomenon and process, affecting every aspect of the day-to-day life of the colonized.
- Colonial violence begins by reorganizing the physical space of the colony, demarcating the 'black' and 'white' town, eventually domesticating nature itself.
- The violence of colonialism dehumanizes the native, making him lose his sense of Self.
- This dehumanization begins when the black man is simply treated as a black body, and is trained to be ashamed of it. There is no attempt to engage with anything deeper than the colour of the skin, argues Fanon.
- This dehumanization and alienation of the Self results in hysteria among the colonized, as rage and frustration build up.
- From losing his sense of Self, and of becoming just an object to the white man, the colonized then also loses his cultural moorings and cultural identity because he begins to be ashamed of his cultural practices and beliefs in a case of cultural trauma.

Fanon's reading of colonial violence, as should be clear from the above summary, is carefully graded. He suggests a trajectory of violence:

the body of the colonized

↓

the psyche of the colonized

↓

the culture of the colonized

Colonialism, therefore, first targets the individual body, then the psyche and finally, the culture itself. The *cumulative* effect of this trajectory of violence, Fanon demonstrates, is the complete destruction, individually and collectively, of the colonized's mind, dignity and culture. We can now examine Fanon's arguments about violence in detail.

Colonialism, emphasizes Fanon, is primarily a state of violence. Every aspect of life for the colonized is subject to endless violence, and all relations between colonizer and colonized are violent. Violence is also what the colonial master uses to ensure the continual obedience of the colonized. Fanon was concerned with various forms of violence. He explored the hard, physical violence of colonial rule, the corporeal mani-festations of this violence, the cultural domination through education, the violence of the language used when talking about/to the natives, and the biomedical field (especially psychiatry), which he treated as a sophisticated form of violence against the native but one cast in the form of scientism.

Fanon sees the colonial system as perpetuating violence on the black at multiple levels. This results in a deeply fractured self with no moorings, stability, or sense of identity. The inferiority complex of the black, writes Fanon, is the result of a 'double process': primarily economic but also the internalization, or what he calls 'epidermalization', of this inferiority (*Black Skin*: 4).

TERRITORY, GEOGRAPHY AND THE VIOLENCE OF SPACE

Colonial violence is initiated with an act of geographical-spatial violence: the physical separation of the world of the colonizer (what Fanon terms 'enemy territory', *Wretched*: 80) from that of the colonized. The colonial world is a compartmentalized world: 'the colonized world is a world divided in two. The dividing line, the border, is represented by the barracks and the police stations' (*Wretched:* 3). The colonial world is ordered, peaceful and neat, while the world of the colonized is 'a world with no space, people are piled one on top of the other, the shacks squeezed tightly together' (4). The colonized's sector is a 'famished sector, hungry for bread, meat, shoes, coal, and light' (4). The colonization of the land through technology or European modernization renders it unrecognizable, except for the bush and jungle. This dual nature of all spaces – whether geographical or demographic – is central to the very condition of colonialism.

The territorial violence of colonialism is a reordering of the land that the natives have used for generations. It divides people arbitrarily, often making deep divisions between people who have coexisted for a long time. In a powerful passage in *Maps* (1999) Somalian novelist Nuruddin Farah (b. 1945) describes geographical colonial violence:

> Someone else insisted that passengers be told where the "inexistent" border used to be – inexistent, because Somalis never admitted it … Non-Somalis, because they were total strangers or knew no better, looked at maps, where they found a curvy line, drawn to cut one Somali people from another.
>
> (Farah 1999: 132)

Nigerian playwright and poet Wole Soyinka also points to the geographical violence of colonialism that divides people:

> I accept that entity, Nigeria, as a space into which I happen to have been born, and therefore a space within which I am bound to collaborate with fellow occupants in the pursuit of justice and ethical life. Expressions such as 'territorial integrity' and the 'sacrosanctity of boundaries,' those relics of colonial master-slave bequest that abjectly glorify the diktat of colonial powers, are meaningless in such a context.
>
> (Soyinka 1996: 133)

This geographical violence results in cultural alienation as well, as Farah's text and Soyinka's statement seems to suggest. Congolese philosopher, novelist and critic V. Y. Mudimbe (b. 1941) echoes Fanon when he notes that colonization was the 'domination of physical space, the reformation of the natives' minds, and the integration of local economic histories into the Western perspective' (Mudimbe 1988: 2).

Nature itself, Fanon suggests, is domesticated and colonized, and is accompanied by the colonization of culture and even imaginations. Signs of colonial authority such as the barracks, the police station, frontiers and their barriers, and hospitals dot the landscape. The construction of railroads and the draining of the swamps alter the topography. Such a transformation of the land is treated as its modernization, where all development is deemed to stem from the white man (*Wretched*: 182). These are acts of violence as well.

In *Black Skin*, Fanon also uses a *spatial* trope to signify both colonial colour prejudice and its propensity for violence. Speaking of this psychiatric experience, Fanon describes the claustrophobic condition of being trapped by his skin colour: 'I was walled in' (*Black Skin*: 89). The 'fact of blackness' is a spatial reality as well: the black body's skin is the boundary that also determines the social boundaries in the colonial situation. Fanon recounts how he was constantly referred to only as the 'Negro physician' or the 'Negro teacher'. It was the colour of his skin and not his 'refined manners ... knowledge of literature, or ... understanding of the quantum theory' that 'marked' him (89). The skin is thus a trap, a confined space from which there is no escape. He finds himself 'sealed into that crushing objecthood' (82), into 'thingness' (170). This is how the black man always sees himself: always in unfavourable comparison with something else. This comparison, for Fanon, occurs at the level of spaces occupied, including the spaces of the body and skin.

EMBODIED VIOLENCE AND THE ALIENATION OF THE SELF

Colonial violence takes a corporeal, physical form. In an unforgettable and haunting passage in *Black Skin,* Fanon writes:

> I had to meet the white man's eyes. An unfamiliar weight burdened me. In the white world the man of color encounters difficulties in the development of his bodily schema. I was battered down by tom-toms, cannibalism, intellectual deficiency, fetishism, racial defects. I took myself far off from my own presence. What else could it be for me but an amputation, an excision, a haemorrhage that spattered my whole body with black blood?

(*Black Skin*: 84–5)

Fanon here powerfully foregrounds trauma first as violence upon the black *body* as a 'racial epidermal' schema (84). The identity of the black is confined to and written upon the colour of the skin. The skin, the surface of the body, becomes the key focus of a racialized identity (Gauch 2002). The white man sees only the black skin, it becomes the foundation for all colonial relations. The black man is reduced to his skin and body, there is no depth, only surface.

The embodied nature of colonial violence and the inscription of racist colonial discourse upon the black man's body was a major concern for Fanon. The black body in Fanon's reading is fragmented, dissolved and exploded (Prabhu 2006). Commenting on the use of torture by French police on Algerian revolutionaries, Fanon suggests that such sadistic measures are intrinsic to the very nature of the occupant–occupied relationship (*African*: 66). Violence upon the body, then, is the hallmark of the colonial condition. Each body, white or black, is 'sealed into his own peculiarity' (*Black Skin*: 31) in the colonial situation. When the black man is forced to see himself through the eyes of the white man the result is the loss of the sense of self: 'The arrival of the white man in Madagascar shattered not only its horizons but its psychological mechanisms' (*Black Skin*: 72). The black body becomes an object rather than a feeling-thinking body, soulless and open to violation in the colonial scheme of things.

The white man's vision literally breaks up the black man's body and, as a result, the black who sees himself through the white man's eyes sees himself as fractured and dismembered – a condition of 'nausea' (*Black Skin:* 84; on Fanon's nausea, see Ahluwalia 2003). This nausea is of 'dislocation' (Fanon's term), a feeling of revulsion at one's self because one has been rejected, as Fanon puts it, 'hated, despised, detested' by an entire race (*Black Skin:* 89). The nausea is a feeling of complete alienation from one's Self because one has been rejected by the white man. The nauseated black body experiences a massive upheaval, and it results in a crisis of identity. It is, therefore, in the white man's *gaze* that the nausea of the black man emerges. The black man is now aware of himself only as a despicable black body. (This emphasis on the white man's gaze that constructs the black man as a black body and nothing more is akin, critics have suggested, to the way the male gaze constructs the female as a mere body: see Bergner 1995.) This nausea is the consequence of colonialism's psychic violence. It results in the annihilation of the black Self.

White psychiatric practices, Fanon notes, often diagnose and pronounce such colonized Africans as 'hysterical'. However, such a diagnosis relies entirely on psychoanalysis, and ignores, in Fanon's reading, the social conditions of the hysteria. 'Hysteria', he argues, is a bodily manifestation of an alienated psyche. The images and signs that constitute the black man's hysteria are signifiers of very real and painful encounters with colonialism's violent racial situations (Gordon 2006: 15). Fanon suggests that the bodily spasms and contortions are 'outlets' for the tortured self (*Wretched*: 19). He proposes that the colonized needs to find some means of expending his frustrated, annihilating psychic energies. Fanon sees tribal and community dances as offering a way out of this high-pressure situation where rage against the colonial master finds expression. The rage, writes Fanon, is 'channeled, transformed and spirited away'. Such dances may involve symbolic killings and extreme violence, but are essentially one of the few modes of expression available to the colonized (19–20).

What Fanon examines here is the mechanism of coping with colonial domination. It is interesting that Fanon locates these mechanisms in tribalisms and local cultural practices, because eventually it is the retrieval of these practices that constitute a cultural nationalism as well. Violence therefore fuels the return to native articulations/expressions such as dance, voodoo and music. Many of these practices and rituals might be forgotten (*Wretched*: 20), but could be drawn upon for purposes of nationalism – a project that characterizes the postcolonial state.

HEGEMONY, VIOLENCE AND CULTURAL TRAUMA

> Everything I say this monkey does do,
> I don't know what to say this monkey won't do.
> I sit down, monkey sit down too,
> I don't know what to say this monkey won't do.

This is Lestrade speaking about the native Makak's mimicking of the white man's ways in Derek Walcott's *Dream on Monkey Mountain* (1970: 223). It captures with savage ferocity the contempt of the colonial master for the colonized who seeks to be as white as possible, but ends up becoming an object of ridicule. This mimicry is the consequence of the violent erasure of native culture in colonialism, and the resultant cultural trauma experienced by the colonized.

> Cultural trauma occurs when members of a collective feel they have been subjected to a horrendous event that leaves an indelible mark upon their group consciousness (Alexander 2004: 1). It is a loss of identity for an entire community.

In *The Chant of Jimmie Blacksmith* Jimmie discovers that his community's old ways of life have been corrupted by colonialism:

> What did Tullam and Mungara stand for now? Tribal men were beggars puking Hunter River rotgut sherry in the lee of hotel shit-houses. Tribal elders, who cared for initiation teeth and knew where the soil-stones of each man were hidden and how the stones could be distinguished, lent out their wives to white men for a suck from a brandy bottle.
>
> (Keneally 1973: 7)

Native cultures, as can be seen from both Walcott's and Keneally's descriptions, were rotting with mimic men, natives with no sense of dignity and the loss of cultural identity itself. Fanon offers a definition of cultural trauma in 'Racism and Culture':

> We witness the destruction of cultural values, of ways of life. Language, dress, techniques, are devalorized … The social panorama is destructed; values are flaunted, crushed, emptied … a new system of values is imposed.
>
> (*African*: 33–4)

The 'inferior' colonized is constructed through a systematic and violent process of hegemonic domination through cultural apparatus such as 'books, newspapers, schools and their texts, advertisements, films, radio' (*Black Skin*: 118; Ian Baucom, 2001, has pointed to the significance Fanon attaches to the radio, but also to listening and voices). In *Wretched*, Fanon argues that the violence of the colonial situation is 'brought into the home and mind of the native' by intermediaries (*Wretched*: 4). The values, beliefs and prejudices of the white cultures are transplanted into African nations and minds to effect cultural domination. The colonized race's collective unconscious equates black skins with ugliness, sin and darkness. There can be no moral black, argues Fanon, because the colonizing stereotype and ways of thinking have convinced the black man he is immoral (*Black Skin*: 148–9). The result is a forcible deculturation of the colonized.

Fanon thus sees the violence on the land, black bodies and psyche (discussed above) as contiguous with the violence perpetrated culturally. Here Fanon shifts his analysis of violence from its physical form to violence as hegemony and as *cultural trauma*. Fanon argues that psychic and individual violence is only a narrower version of larger, cultural violence perpetrated at the level of the entire colonized society. Numerous postcolonial writers have recognized this (Fanonian) condition of cultural trauma.

Kenyan activist-novelist Ngũgĩ wa Thiong'O (b. 1938) in *The River Between* writes: 'the white man had come to Siriana, and Joshua and Kabonyi had been converted. They had abandoned the ridges and followed the new faith' (1965: 5). In the Zimbabwean Tsitsi Dangarembga's (b. 1959) *Nervous Conditions*, Nhamo, who leaves the ancestral village, realizes that, when he comes home, he is unable to deal with his native culture anymore. 'The poverty', writes Dangarembga, 'begins to offend him' (1988: 7). Elesin in Wole Soyinka's *Death and the King's Horseman* is categorical in his denunciation of colonial violence on the colonized's culture and psyche: '[It] turned me into an infant in the hands of unnamable strangers … My will was squelched in the spittle of an alien race' (1984: 211–12). Ngũgĩ, Dangarembga and Soyinka all point to the disruption of a way of life and the consequent cultural trauma of alienation. The 'squelched will' is the annihilation of the self in colonialism.

One major domain in which this cultural trauma occurs, in Fanon's reading, is language. Fanon argues that the very identity of the black man depends on his ability to acquire fluency in the colonizer's language. He writes: 'The Negro of the Antilles will be proportionately whiter – that is, he will come closer to being a real human being – in direct ratio to his mastery of the French language' (*Black Skin:* 8). And later: 'To speak a language is to take on a world, a culture. The Antilles Negro who wants to be white will be the whiter as he gains greater mastery of the cultural tool that language is' (25). This theme of the European language as a cultural weapon that destroys the native is again a common theme in postcolonial literature.

Fanon seems to anticipate postcolonial writers like Rushdie, Caribbean-British V. S. Naipaul (b. 1932) and Soyinka, who satirize the formerly colonized who stay nostalgically rooted in colonial times/cultures:

> No spectacular undertaking will make us forget the legalized racism, the
> illiteracy, the flunkeyism generated and maintained in the very depth of the
> consciousness of our people.
>
> *(African:* 101)

Fanon is addressing the legacy of colonialism here. In Salman Rushdie's
Midnight's Children (1981), the Methwold Estate is full of mimic men
and women. Here Indians seek perfect British accents and live in
houses called 'Buckingham', 'Sans Souci', 'Escorial' and 'Versailles' as
Rushdie mocks the colonized's desire to be more white than white.
The very consciousness of the people, Rushdie suggests, has been
altered by contact with the colonizer's culture. In the previous chapter
we have already cited Soyinka's satiric take in *Death and the King's
Horseman* on the natives who wish to speak and act like their colonial
masters. In V. S. Naipaul's *The Middle Passage* we see this legacy in the
formerly colonized's abandonment of their cultures and the mimicking
of their former European masters. Naipaul describes Trinidadians and
their deculturation thus:

> A peasant-minded, money-minded community, spiritually cut off from its roots,
> its religion reduced to rites without philosophy set in a materialistic colonial
> society: a combination of historical accidents and national temperament has
> turned the Trinidad Indian into a complete colonial, even more Philistine than
> the white.
>
> (1969: 89)

(Ironically, globalization has resulted in a similar mimicry as young
Indian men and women, with assumed western names, carefully
acquired American accents and cultural information, telephonically
serve American customers at call centers in India; see Shome 2006.)
In another work, *The Enigma of Arrival*, Naipaul describes how, when
he was younger, he had images of the 'lowing herd winding o'er the
lea' from the English poet Thomas Gray's famous poem 'Elegy Written
in a Country Churchyard', while his idea of a cow was that of the
animals pictured on condensed milk-cans, even though no such herds
existed on his island of Trinidad (1987: 38, 80, 297). This serves to
exemplify the violent invasion by western culture of the consciousness
and imagination of the natives, so that they can now only talk, think
and even dream *like* westerners.

We see an example of such a deculturation in Jeanette Armstrong's 'This is a Story' (1996). White settlers build dams over the rivers in Canada as a result of which salmon migration, the principal source of food for the natives, ends. The natives then start eating the white man's food. Kyoti, the protagonist of Armstrong's tale, treats this 'incorporation' of the white man's food as indicative of the loss of native culture itself as they (the natives) assimilate the colonizer's culture. Armstrong, like Soyinka, Dangarembga, Ngũgĩ and Naipaul, is concerned with the violent 'deculturation' of the native with the arrival of colonialism. When the natives start thinking in the language of the white, when they ingest the food/culture of the colonizer, they simply stop being black or brown: they become deracinated and 'white-like', so to speak. Even when the black man – the native intellectual – seeks to speak out against colonialist thought, he is unable to think/speak outside the terrain already mapped out to him, a terrain that is 'continental' and 'national' rather than local and tribal. Fanon calls this total domination of the black man's thinking a 'racialization of thought' (*Wretched*: 150). It is this cultural alienation that Fanon sees as the heart of colonial violence.

Fanon argues – and we see here a now-established theme in post-colonial theory – the following:

- Colonial domination was possible because of a violent reductionism, where the colonized was reduced to stereotypes of evil (a 'quintessence of evil', as he puts it in *Wretched*: 6), freezing the native in a static mould;
- This reductionism, in turn, dehumanizes the native: he is made to feel like an animal because he is addressed, described and believed to be an animal by the colonial apparatus.

Fanon notes:

> He [the colonizer] speaks of the yellow man's reptilian motions, of the stink of the native quarter, of breeding swarms, of foulness, of spawn, of gesticulations.
> (*Wretched*: 7)

The act of classifying and naming serves to dehumanize the native into an animal. The demolition of his cultural identity results in the obliteration of his subjectivity: one leads to the other in colonialism. The colonized lack all agency, as individuals and as a culture. This is the cultural trauma of colonialism manifest at the level of both individuals and communities/collectives.

As a result of such persistent violence, the native finds his self being slowly but thoroughly destroyed. Fanon saw colonialism as a condition where the colonized lost all sense of the self, personality and subjectivity, or what he called the 'expulsion of [the] self' (*Dying*: 65). And yet, there emerge modes through which the suppressed anxieties and violence emerge in the colonized. When both the individual self and the collective cultural identity are destroyed by colonial violence a counterviolence will also emerge, Fanon shows, at both levels. It is to this role of violence as a *reconstructive* strategy of the self to which I now turn in the next chapter.

SUMMARY

Fanon's analysis of colonialism focuses on its violence. Colonialism for Fanon was always primarily a violent process, affecting every aspect of the day-to-day life of the colonized. Colonial violence begins by reorganizing the physical space of the colony, demarcating the 'black' and 'white' town, eventually domesticating nature through railways, roads and canals. The colonial apparatus sets about perpetuating violence on the individuals as well. The black man is simply treated as a black body, and is trained to be ashamed of it. There is no attempt to engage with something deeper than the colour of the skin, argues Fanon. Further, there is always the fear of the police, the law and torture – forms of physical violence within colonialism. Together, the embodied and psychological violence results in a dehumanization and alienation of the Self. The colonized now exhibits hysteria, as rage and frustration build up.

Fanon argues that colonial violence does not stop at the individual body and psyche. The colonized eventually also loses his cultural moorings and cultural identity because he begins to be ashamed of his cultural practices and beliefs in a case of cultural trauma. He begins to move away from his cultural practices and adopt those of his master. The dislocation completes the alienation of the colonized: he has lost touch with himself as well as his culture. Western psychiatric practices, Fanon argues, do not acknowledge the colonial violence that produces the native's hysteria.

We have now arrived at the moment where Fanon's key thesis regarding violence may be studied: that the violence of the colonized is a response to the inherent, destructive violence of the colonial system, and that the violence of the colonized is reconstructive in nature. This thesis is the subject of the next chapter.

6

ON VIOLENCE II

The Reconstruction of Selfhood

The preceding chapter examined Fanon's analysis of colonial violence. It demonstrated how colonial violence alters and even destroys the land, the individual body of the colonized and his psyche, and eventually alienates him and his community from their history and culture in a case of cultural trauma. This is the violence that destroys the Self. However, Fanon's critique of violence does not end with this component of violence: he is also interested in the ways in which the colonized is driven to violence as a means of recuperating his Self. This reconstructive-recuperative violence by the colonized is the subject of the present chapter.

'The colonized man liberates himself in and through violence', wrote Fanon in *Wretched* (44). The colonized native, for a long time beaten into the ground, begins to carve out a new Self first in the form of anti-colonial resistance, which takes the form of violence. Thus violence is preceded by a moment of consciousness and awareness where the colonized recognizes his oppression. Once this recognition dawns, then the violent insurrection against the oppressor occurs.

Violence in Fanon, this chapter argues, is directed at two specific goals and corresponds to two kinds of violence (I am adopting here the arguments of Kawash 1999 and Seshadri-Crooks 2002):

1   The first goal is the overthrow of the colonizer in the form of the anti-colonial struggle. The violence of the anti-colonial struggle is

'instrumental violence', and is essentially a social project, directed at the community as a whole.

2   The second goal emerges from the first one. In the process of the anti-colonial struggle, argues Fanon, the colonized's self-realization and the retrieval of subjectivity is achieved. This retrieved subjectivity, dignity and identity, for Fanon, quite possibly leads to death and annihilation. But this annihilation would be one of choice and self-hood rather than abjection, with Fanon arguing that he would be willing to accept 'dissolution' (*Black Skin*: 170). It is in this second mode of violence, directed at self-realization, that Fanon finds the possibilities of a new identity and humanism. This kind of violence seeking a remaking of the Self is 'absolute violence', and is essentially an individual project directed at the individual Self.

If instrumental violence seeks to re-establish the *cultural* identity of the natives which the colonial situation had erased, absolute violence seeks to retrieve a Self that has been buried under the humiliations of the colonial master. The liberated Self with its new subjectivity marks the moment where 'new men' emerge. When such 'new men' gather as a collective it generates a total rupture in the world.

From this newly self-realized native, Fanon suggests towards the end of *Black Skin*, emerges the 'actional' man, where the former slave rediscovers his capacity to love and respect the 'basic values that constitute a human world' (173). Violence therefore becomes the preliminary to (i) a new subjectivity and cultural identity for the black/colonized, and (ii) a new humanism. This is something to be kept in mind: *violence in Fanon is always the route to self-determination and identity formation*. It enables the colonized to generate their self-identity and therefore proceed to build a new social order (Gordon 1995: 71; Roberts 2004: 142–3).

Fanon does not, let us note, emphasize violence for itself. He treats violence as restitution, a response and a liberatory force through which the oppressed colonized can express himself. It is instrumental violence when used in the anti-colonial struggle because it is a *response* to the violence of the white man, and seeks to overthrow the colonial regime. Thus the anti-colonial violence is part of the *dialectic* whose other pole is colonial violence. The entire relationship between white and black was forged in violence; locked into a dialectic of violence by the very nature of the colonial system, the colonized has little option but to use violence in his struggle. Since the relationship was also sustained through violence, the only way it can be broken is through further violence, this time through the violence of the colonized. It is the desperation of the colonial situation – individual and cultural alienation and annihilation – that leads the colonized into violence.

In the first section of this chapter we shall look at the first moment of violence as Fanon explores it: the instrumental anti-colonial violence. In the second section we examine how, in Fanon, the violence of the anti-colonial struggle leads to the formation of a new subjectivity in the colonized.

ANTI-COLONIAL STRUGGLES AND INSTRUMENTAL VIOLENCE

Fanon's views on the necessity of violence in the colonial context include the following key ideas:

- The very nature of the political space in colonialism is extremely skewed and exclusionary (Sekyi-Otu 1996: 87): the African has no role in the political system, which is entirely controlled by the whites and in which the African is only a passive subject.
- Violence is a means of asserting his role in this political space.
- Violence therefore redefines the nature of the political space.

In the context of colonialism, the victim of unrelenting violence himself becomes violent. It becomes his mission to carve out a space for himself, to put himself, if possible, in the settler's position: 'for the colonized, life can only materialize from the rotting cadaver of the colonist' (*Wretched*: 50). Anti-colonial struggles, therefore, represent a 'breaking-out' of the colonized in violence as a mode of attaining a measure of self-hood. This claiming of self-hood is necessary because of the very nature of the political in colonialism.

The political is a relationship between individuals in a community, and between subjects and their representatives/governors. But this relationship has been subverted in the colonial context. The African is completely erased and negated in the colonial system: he has no say in the system of governance, no rights, no claims. Thus, the political space in colonialism does not provide any access for the black subject.

For Fanon, violence becomes a mode of reclaiming that space, or what he terms 'absolute praxis' (*Wretched*: 44). If there is no 'proper' political relationship then the state descends into violence. In other words, the absence of a truly political space would result in recourse to the state of violence.

A violent struggle – what he termed a 'murderous and decisive struggle' against the colonizer, Fanon argued, was the only means of overthrowing the oppressor. Fanon regards this violence as essential to the national project:

> We have said that the violence of the colonized unifies the people. By its very structure, colonialism is separatist and regionalist. Colonialism does not simply state the existence of tribes; it also reinforces it and separates them. The colonial system encourages chieftaincies and keeps alive the old Marabout confraternities. Violence in its practice is totalizing, national. It follows that it is closely involved in the liquidation of regionalism and tribalism. Thus, the nationalist parties show no pity at all toward the caids and the customary chiefs. The liquidation of the caids and the chiefs is the preliminary to the unification of the people.
>
> (*Wretched*: 51)

Fanon is not pleading for violence that establishes a European-Enlightenment model of national identity. He wishes for a liberating violence that ushers in a national identity that supports difference. He does not for a moment consider the European model of nationalism – which he deems totalitarian, homogenizing and therefore violent in itself when led by social elites. The elites, he acknowledges, are not really interested in engaging the masses. Instead, they have their own agenda that wilfully 'tramples over the little local histories' (*Wretched*: 67–8). Instrumental violence therefore dismantles the oppressive structures of not only colonialism but also of old-fashioned humanisms.

Fanon argues that the anti-colonial struggle does not end with the exit of the oppressor. What is essential for a true decolonization (we shall return to decolonization and its processes in the next chapter) is for the formerly colonized to clear their heads of the ideas and myths generated by the colonial. This means that the project of purging the colonial cannot end with the instrumental violence of the anti-colonial struggle. (Fanon assumes, however, that anti-colonial resistance is only through violence. But there were, as James Scott's [1985] study shows, other 'weapons of the weak': pilferage, pretended ignorance, slander, indolence, etc.) It must be carried on into the process of decolonization for the true Self to emerge and from which a new, better humanism is possible. In other words, Fanon sees the instrumental violence of the anti-colonial struggle only as an early step or stage in the retrieval of the Self, the true 'human' within, of the colonized. A second step, in decolonization, is essential as well.

ABSOLUTE VIOLENCE, SELF-REALIZATION AND HUMANISM

Fanon argues that the anti-colonial struggle does not end with the exit of the oppressor. What is essential for a true decolonization is for the formerly colonized to clear their heads of the ideas and myths generated by the colonial (an instance of hegemonic and epistemic violence). 'Absolute violence' (as Kawash, 1999, terms it) therefore:

- exceeds the goal of merely evicting the colonizer;
- seeks a purging of the ideas, myths and notions planted in the colonized by the colonizer – a process we can think of as the decolonization of the mind.

It is only after the colonial master's implanted worldview has been completely erased that a new Self can emerge for the colonized. We could therefore argue that absolute violence has a greater value in Fanonian thought: for this form of violence is truly liberatory in seeking something far more than an immediate goal. The decolonization of the mind is this true liberation.

Fanon suggests a mode of 'unlearning' all the 'untruths planted within him [the black] by the oppressor if a fuller personality has to develop' (*Wretched*: 233). Decolonization is a violent purging of colonial ideas from the mind and imagination of the colonized. This suggests that violence is not merely about exiling the colonial master but ensuring agency and self-determination. This is violence in 'excess' (Kawash 1999: 237) of the instrumental need of the colonized. Fanon locates the possibility of a new subjectivity in this form of violence.

The project of the revival of the Self, thus also demands violence. Violence becomes a means of acquiring a measure of self-respect for the colonized: 'the former slave needs a challenge to his humanity, he wants a conflict, a riot' (*Black Skin*: 172). It helps assert a minimal amount of *agency* in response to a condition of absolute servility and suppression.

Fanon sees violence as both an assertion of agency as well as a means to recover it. Violence here is to be seen as *praxis*, an acting out, or a performance in which the Self is rediscovered. Fanon writes: 'The colonized subject discovers reality and transforms it through his praxis, his deployment of violence and his agenda for liberation' (*Wretched*: 21).

Fanon has already argued that colonialism erases the native's soul, Self and identity. Any praxis or performance that enables and empowers the colonized to *retrieve* a Self, or agency, must therefore be treated as positive. That this praxis/performance is violent is unfortunate, but one which finds its origins in the colonial system itself: it is the violent oppression by the white man that turns the black into a violent person.

When the colonized takes to violence, he finds it liberating, *irrespective* of the goal or consequence of his actions. In Keneally's *The Chant of Jimmie Blacksmith*, the acts of barbaric killing are, Jimmy understands, inhuman. But then Jimmy does not see his violence as world-directed. It is 'intrinsic' because the very act of violence helps him see him-self, find him-self. The violence takes its toll on the world, but ultimately, it is not of or about the world: it is about Jimmy's Self.

That violence is not an end in itself, but directed at something more, is evidenced in statements Fanon makes throughout his writings. Thus in *Dying Colonialism* he writes:

> Because we want a democratic and renovated Algeria, because we believe one cannot rise and liberate oneself in one area and sink in another, we condemn with pain in our hearts, those brothers who have flung themselves into revolutionary action with the almost physiological brutality that centuries of oppression give rise to and feed.
>
> (*Dying*: 25)

'Hatred', Fanon declares elsewhere, is 'not an agenda' (*Wretched*: 89). But if hatred and violence are to be the basis for a whole new politics, how is a humanist politics and humanism to emerge from such a condition of conflict and strife? This question has been at the forefront of considerable Fanon scholarship.

Self-realization and cultural realization are dependent upon each other, in Fanon's view. Colonization destroys a community, a culture and the individual. It erases the Self, denies agency and annihilates a tradition. The violence of decolonization, Fanon suggests, retrieves precisely this:

1 annihilated cultural tradition;
2 dormant history;
3 fractured Self through agential violence.

What is clear is that for Fanon *both* individual and cultural-communitarian selfhood can be retrieved through absolute violence.

The individual acting out his violence, the violent dances of the colonized and the community's cultural nationalism are all to be treated, in Fanon, as *agential*. The 'actional' man with a 'respect for the basic values that constitute a human world' (*Black Skin*: 173) is the starting point for a new humanism. Fanon rejects the *individualist humanism of the western world for the collectivism of African and Asian cultures*. The formerly colonized individual now finds a new subjectivity, and the nation itself finds a new destiny and a 'collective history' (*Wretched*: 51). Sometimes, of course, this retrieval of a collective history, a return to one's culture and the self-enlightenment demanded of the formerly colonized is itself a violent act. We see a particularly horrific example of this form of decolonization in Wole Soyinka's *Death and the King's Horseman*.

Olunde, the King's horseman, Elesin's son, has been educated in the west and has therefore become some sort of cultural renegade. Elesin himself had abandoned his vocation, and backed out of the traditional suicide ritual he is supposed to perform. Olunde now seeks reparation, from himself. When Elesin refuses to commit ritual suicide, Olunde is the one who seeks to restore the pride of his culture and family, and thus kills himself. The praise-singer, sitting beside the body and an Elesin racked with grief, says to him:

> There lies the honour of your household and of our race. Because he could not bear to let honour fly out of doors, he stopped it with his life. The son has proved the father, Elesin, and there is nothing left in your mouth to gnash but infant gums.
>
> (1984: 218)

Decolonization, which involves a return to cultural roots and belief systems, is here violent, and marks a collective pride in its heritage, even when purchased at the cost of one's life. This sacrifice, the praise-singer suggests, is the marker of a new identity for the entire race/ tribe/community from which emerges the new identity of the individual. This renewed Elesin identity is rooted in his culture and community.

Fanon locates the new subjectivity of the individual (manifest in Olunde's death, and the praise-singer's evaluation of it as an act that redeems the community's pride within the tribe/group) within a collective context of consciousness and political awareness. The liberated individual is not 'an island'. In Fanon's formulation, 'the violence of the colonized ... unifies the people' (*Wretched*: 51), even when the violence is self-directed and self-destructive, as in the case of Olunde. For Fanon the brutal conditions of colonialism necessitate a new humanism. When colonialism is overthrown what is also rejected is Eurocentric humanism (a humanism characterized by paternalistic benevolence, tolerance and identity politics, which gives no agency to the 'less-than-human' black). It urges the thus-far 'subhuman' black to acquire western humanity, argues Fanon (*Wretched*: 110). Fanon here rejects Western/European humanism treating it as complicit with racism and colonialism (Young 1990: 122. But Young also wonders if it is possible to develop a non-conflictual humanism such as the one Fanon proposes, where the human is no longer theorized or constructed in opposition to the non- or sub-human, 1990: 125).

In other words, what Fanon proposes is that violence results in agency, and agency is central to the:

1 imagination of a different social order;
2 construction of a new politics itself.

Decolonizing violence liberates both the individual and the society, and this is precisely why violence becomes the preliminary moment of a new humanism. It marks a rupture in colonial and colonizing ways of thinking, behaviour and human relations. Decolonization, which we shall examine in greater detail in a later chapter, is therefore the *rejection of western humanism as well as western colonialism*. A formerly colonized individual and society who/that has liberated him-/itself will redefine thinking, behaviour and human relations. This view of violence as transformational and preliminary to the making of a new social order is given to us very early in the essay on violence when Fanon writes:

> It [decolonization] infuses a new rhythm, specific to a new generation of men, with a new language and a new humanity. Decolonization is truly the creation of new men.
>
> (*Wretched*: 3)

It requires a (violent) evacuation of European ideas and beliefs. Fanon was clear that decolonization was possible only when the formerly colonized truly abandoned European ways of thinking. Fanon argues that 'for many among us [colonized] the European model is the most inspiring' (*Wretched*: 236), and we thus remain intellectually colonized as well. This argument is borne out by the continual economic imperialism and western models of 'development' that are imposed (through the nefarious Structural Adjustment Programs, trade embargoes and organizations such as the WTO) on formerly colonized nations. Writing from Egypt, Nawal El Saadawi notes, for instance:

> Development ... is visualized as a process of cultural change, of modernization along the lines of Western life, of technological advance which would permit better utilization of resources.
>
> (1980: i–ii)

Decolonization therefore is greater than anti-colonial struggles. Fanon writes: 'let us decide not to imitate Europe; let us combine our muscles and our brains in a new direction' (*Wretched*: 236). 'Muscles and brains', indicating both physical action and intellectual activity, are both equally important to free the formerly colonized fully from the clutches of the European.

Not for Fanon the western model of humanism where the white man was the measure of all things. Fanon writes in 'Racism and Culture': 'universality resides in this decision to recognise and accept the reciprocal relativism of different cultures, once the colonial status is irreversibly excluded' (*African*: 44). The decolonized 'new man' will recognize and respect difference. We see Fanon here already moving towards a form of universality, of mutual recognition that would, in his view, produce a new humanism. The liberated human recognizes difference because he has just achieved, through a violent assertion of the Self, the recognition of/for his own difference: I am not white, but black, I am not a thing but a man. It is in this transformational power of violence – which creates new subjectivities sensitive to suffering and difference – that Fanon detects the chances of a new humanism.

For Fanon, violence leads to what Sidi Omar has termed 'psychic redemption' (2009: 270. Parallels have been drawn between Fanon's emphasis on such redemptive violence and African American writer-activist Richard Wright's views on the same, see Wilmot 2009). Yet it is not the psychic redemption of an individual in which Fanon is interested, but a cultural redemption and therefore a new humanity that has recovered from the debilitating effects of colonialism. Violence that results from colonial domination thus becomes a mode of retrieval of the Self. It is from this retrieved self – individual as well as collective – that Fanon hopes a new humanism might emerge.

In the late twentieth-century arguments over human rights, especially in the western world, have presupposed an autonomous, self-willed individual, able to act as a free agent (Ignatieff 2001; Slaughter 2007). If human rights are based on this condition of possessing agency, then a preliminary step would be to ensure conditions in which such an agent would emerge. As we have seen, Fanon sees the colonial condition as one in which the native individual is simply wiped out, without culture or consciousness. Such an individual is not a full 'person', but rather a passive subject with no sense of Self. For an individual to become truly aware of his Self, he needs to escape the colonial condition. He has to be aware of his Self so that he can choose his life hereafter, pursue a plot of his life. Freedom is this freedom to choose, and is based on the awareness of the Self.

Fanon suggests that the colonized becomes a free agent through these acts of violence. He writes in *Black Skin*: 'Self-consciousness accepts the risk of its life, and consequently it threatens the other in his physical being' (169). Violence as a means of discovery of the Self and therefore the emergence of the autonomous individual (free of structures like colonialism) is therefore an anterior moment to the rise of the subject of human rights itself. Such an individual is capable of self-determination, and is therefore the appropriate subject of human rights.

Absolute violence, therefore, in Fanon's thinking follows this trajectory and has these consequences:

- It enables the individual to retrieve a sense of Self, of self-worth, as a person capable of achieving something through *action*.
- It helps him decolonize his mind when the colonized becomes more aware of himself *and* his cultural identity.

- Because of this awareness he in effect *returns* to his culture and community while abandoning the European's.
- Such a reformed, or transformed, community serves as a new social order imbued with a new humanism.
- This new humanism is more inclusive, and collective, and rejects the individualist humanism of the European.

SUMMARY

Fanon's conceptualization of violence, this chapter argued, points to two kinds of violence directed at two different but related goals. The first is the violence of the anti-colonial struggle, an 'instrumental violence'. This is essentially a social project, directed at the community as a whole. Violence is a means of asserting the colonized's role in the colonial political space that denies him any voice. Violence is therefore a means of entering this racist and discriminatory political space.

The second is 'absolute violence' through which the colonized's self-realization and the retrieval of subjectivity is achieved. This retrieved subjectivity and identity might lead to death and annihilation. But this annihilation would be one of choice and therefore is a mark of selfhood. It is in this second mode of violence, directed at self-realization, that Fanon finds the possibilities of a new identity and humanism. This kind of violence that seeks a remaking of the Self is essentially an individual project directed at the individual self. Here the violence exceeds the goal of merely evicting the colonizer and seeks a purging of the ideas, myths and notions planted in the colonized by the colonizer – a decolonization of the mind. It thus enables him to get back to his culture, and his community, and when others do the same, the community itself is transformed. Such a reformed, or transformed, community serves as a new social order imbued with a new humanism.

Violence, therefore, is the route to (i) self-retrieval and (ii) cultural retrieval. This cultural retrieval and rebuilding of the community by an erasure of the colonial intellectual legacy is decolonization. Decolonization, so central to the postcolonial nation/culture, is the subject of the next chapter.

7

DECOLONIZATION

There is nothing disgraceful about the African weather ... the palm tree is a fit
subject for poetry.

Achebe ('The Novelist as Teacher', 1965, cited in Ngwarsungu 1990)

In the heady days of the anti-British struggle in India, Lokamanya
Balgangadhar Tilak (1856–1920), a prominent political leader, hit upon
an innovative idea of uniting the communities in the Bombay Presidency.
On the occasion of the annual festivities for the Hindu god Ganesha, he
restored the procession and public celebrations. The spectacle of the
idols and the frenzied crowds served a crucial purpose: they became a
rallying point for Hindus. Tilak used a religious and cultural event to
generate communitarian public feelings. He showed how cultural
practices could be effectively harnessed for nationalist purposes. From
a different context, Ngũgĩ wa Thiong'O notes how during the Mau
Mau anticolonial struggle (1952–60) against the British in Kenya
(which eventually led to Kenyan independence):

> They [the freedom fighters] rediscovered the old songs – they had never
> completely lost touch with them – and reshaped them to meet the new needs
> of their struggle. They also created new songs and dances with new rhythms
> where the old ones were found inadequate.

(1972: 30)

What Achebe states as a literary manifesto, what Tilak performed and Ngũgĩ wa Thiong'O recalls of the Mau Mau freedom fighters, were *spectacles* of what postcolonial theory recognizes as a component of anti-colonial struggles: cultural nationalism. Folklore, oral cultures, music and dance that recalled a precolonial past served the purpose of igniting nationalist sentiments, and Fanon recognized the significance of cultural nationalism in the process of both anti-colonial struggle *and* decolonization.

> Decolonization is a process through which nations in Africa, Asia and South America which have acquired political independence from European nations (whose colonies they had been) also seek to attain intellectual and cultural independence from European thought and ideas. Colonialism had implanted European myths and ideas in the colonized through education, religion and the law. It had also destroyed the native's belief in his/her culture, and in many cases, erased those practices. Decolonization is part of a process of retrieving those cultural practices and belief in them, to get back to native, local and pre-colonial ways of thinking. Decolonization is mainly an intellectual project.

Decolonization, as the explanation in the box suggests, is the attempt to reverse colonial conditions. One of the most significant aspects of decolonization had to do, in Fanon's reading, with the question of culture. (Fanon, however, did believe that some form of economic reparation for the formerly colonized, and a more equitable distribution of the wealth of the nations, was legitimate in decolonization, *Wretched*: 59. For a commentary, see Buck 2004.) Decolonization involves restoring a measure of pride in the colonized's culture – what is called cultural nationalism.

This chapter studies Fanon's writings on decolonization and cultural nationalism under two main heads:

- the retrieval of a national culture where pride is taken in 'negritude' so that a 'black consciousness' is made possible, enabling the colonized to acquire a sense of the Self as a *black human* Self;
- the role intellectuals play in producing this consciousness among the peasants and the masses.

BLACK CONSCIOUSNESS, NEGRITUDE AND NATIONAL CULTURE

A national consciousness and pride in native cultures, Fanon along with several others of his time argued, was central to both anti-colonial struggles and decolonization. Central to this consciousness for Algerians and other Africans was negritude.

NEGRITUDE

Aimé Césaire's *Discourse on Colonialism* declared: 'We adopted the word *nègres* as a term of defiance' (1972: 29). Yet it served as more than a term: it indicated a change of attitude itself, where the black abandoned the apologetic stance towards his culture and began to take pride in it. Césaire saw negritude as the rise of black consciousness, not a static 'thing' but a dynamic process of transformation: the black man accepts his blackness and begins to be proud of it. After Césaire, the Senegalese poet, essayist, politician and Senegal's first president, Leopold Senghor (1906–2001), converted negritude into a political ideology and weapon and thus linked subjective, individual feelings with racial consciousness.

Fanon saw black consciousness as something that:

- enables the colonized to transcend the psyche imposed on him ('I am a black thing' – see Chapter 5 on colonial violence for Fanon's analysis of the destruction of the colonized's Self) by colonialism and therefore;
- enables the making of self-consciousness and finally;
- enables the colonized to see his Self as connected to his *racial* and therefore communitarian identity. He is now able to say: 'I am a black human being'.

Black consciousness is a retreat from the colonial conditions where the colonized's consciousness has been invaded by the white man's. Since the white man (the other) chose not to recognize the black, argued Fanon, there remained only one solution open to the black: to make himself known as a *black man* (*Black Skin*: 87). It is primarily a *self-consciousness*.

Negritude enables self-consciousness and thus the *start* of rediscovery: of the black's humanity. Colonialism had rendered the black an object, dehumanized him, and negritude foregrounds the black man as *human*.

(Later, Fanon would argue that there was a need to go beyond negritude and racial identity itself.) This self-consciousness is then the starting point, a stage, in the rediscovery of the Self, but is also connected to his *racial* identity.

Black consciousness is a three-step process, which involves:

- the rise of self-consciousness and freedom from a relational identity where 'black' was always seen in relation to 'white';
- the repudiation of white beliefs, values and thinking;
- the retrieval of one's native beliefs, values and thinking.

Let us take each of these steps in turn.

First, colonialism annihilates the Self. In the absence of any recognition or validation from the white man, the black man develops a sense of worthlessness. Even labour does not bring the black man a sense of self-worth. The slave is set free by the master, but the slave does not find self-worth in this because he has not *fought* for his freedom (*Black Skin*: 169). But Fanon sees the newly self-conscious black as being able to transcend the psyche imposed on the black by the colonial context. Fanon refuses to see this as only 'potential'. 'My Negro consciousness ... does not hold itself out as a lack. It *is*. It is its own follower' (103, emphasis in original).

Fanon argues that the dialectic of colonialism (master–slave, white–black, superior–inferior) generates the black identity: the black man is made aware that he is just black. That is, during colonialism, the black man was only seen in relation to the white man, and that too as a negative, or a lack: 'not-white'. As Fanon puts it, 'it is not I who make a meaning for myself, but it is the meaning that was already there, pre-existing, waiting for me' (*Black Skin*: 102). Now the black wishes to generate a meaning for himself, as himself, and *not* in relation to the white man. The black man needs an identity *in his own right*, as himself, not in comparison or in contrast with the white man (here Fanon is disputing Sartre's famous claim that 'negritude appears as the minor term of a dialectical progression' (quoted in *Black Skin*: 101)). He frees himself of the white–black dialectic. Black self-consciousness in this second stage is (i) identical with itself, (ii) does not seek a dialectic or external validation, coming to it through a confrontation with violence, and (iii) is always a racial consciousness: of being not only a Self, but a *black* self. *Self-consciousness, in other words, is race or black consciousness: negritude.*

Once the black individual situates himself within the collective, or racial, identity, a return to black culture is ensured – the third step in the negritude process. Black consciousness here is at once individual and collective. To accept negritude is to be within a racial group identity as well. Once a self-consciousness has emerged it results in a *national* consciousness, and national consciousness is a key component of decolonization because it rejects the colonial culture and seeks to return to a local, native one.

However, Fanon is also quick to note that a self-consciousness that is rooted in the black experience is aware that the 'negro experience is not a whole, for there is not merely *one* Negro, there are *Negroes*' (*Black Skin*: 104, emphasis in original). Fanon calls for the recognition of diversity and difference. It is this recognition, as we shall see, that constitutes the emergence of a new humanism.

NATIONAL CULTURE

In Ngũgĩ's *A Grain of Wheat* (1967), the freedom fighter Kihika tries to inspire his fellow countrymen to fight by calling upon ancestral wisdom (represented in Swahili proverbs) as well as the Bible. Kihika represents the intellectual who makes use of local and native resources as a means of arousing consciousness, by appealing to a shared thought process. This is the making of a national culture.

Fanon defines national culture as a 'collective thought process' of a people ('On National Culture', *Wretched*: 168). This transformative 'collective thought process' implies an education of the masses through particular kinds of cultural expressions such as poetry or artisanship.

National culture or cultural nationalism has three main uses, according to Fanon:

- It generates continuity with a community's past.
- It alerts the colonized to colonialism's agenda of 'ensnaring' them to Western culture (*Wretched*: 148).
- It helps retrieve those cultural practices that the colonial regime had sought to erase or reject.

National cultures thus help restore pride and a measure of confidence that had been seriously and severely eroded by colonialism. Fanon thus sees national cultures as a *psychological* necessity (*Wretched*: 148). In

Black Skin he had argued that the black colonized can only confront the condition of slavery through a retreat into the precolonial past. Hence a consciousness – individual as well as collective – of the past is essential (*Black Skin*: 106).

This is very evidently a cultural vision, where the recognition of the *culture of colonialism* – the oppression, the annihilation of the Self, the inferiority complex, the dependency and the violence – enables both the colonized and the colonizer to break free of the neurosis. Both colonizer and colonized become 'cultural subjects' (Stephan Feuchtwang's term 1987: 127). What is fascinating about Fanon's arguments regarding cultural nationalism is that he sees anti-colonial struggles as liberating both the colonizer and the colonized. The black discovers his cultural heritage (of slavery but also of his African past) and the white man discovers that 'that he is at once the perpetrator and the victim of a delusion' (*Black Skin*: 175).

National cultures and cultural nationalism involved the invocation of mythic, mystic and sometimes historically accurate pasts. Narratives from nineteenth-century India such as Bankim Chandra Chatterjee's novel, *Anandamath* (1882), for example, projected Hindu traditions and cultures as authentic India, even sweeping away the Muslim past. Bankim's cultural nationalism therefore pitted *Hindu* culture against both Islamic and English 'colonialisms'. Here anti-colonialism takes the form of a cultural nationalism in which one cultural-historical line of thought and practice – Hinduism – is expanded into a 'national' culture.

Fanon treats negritude as a form of cultural nationalism that appeared *across* Africa. He writes: 'Busia from Ghana, Birago Diop from Senegal, Hampate Ba from Mali and Saint-Clair Drake from Chicago were quick to claim common ties and identical lines of thought' (*Wretched*: 151). He notes how Arab nationalism was inextricably linked to the rise of interest in Islamic cultures (151). Fanon praises Arab revival for seeking an identity beyond the national: 'Their actual cultural experience is not national but Arab' (152). Likewise, Fanon hopes for an African cultural identification rather than a narrow nation-based one. That is, while Fanon sees cultural nationalism as a unificatory force, he is also careful to emphasize that 'culture' cannot be narrowly defined but must be broad-based. Fanon writes:

> The African intellectuals who are still fighting in the name of 'Negro-African' culture and who continue to organize conferences dedicated to the unity of

> that culture should realize that they can do little more than compare coins and sarcophagi.
>
> (*Wretched*: 168)

Fanon is clear that there cannot be identical cultures, or closed ones. For national cultures to develop, one must look at *shared* conditions of colonialism:

> There is no common destiny between the national cultures of Guinea and Senegal, but there is a common destiny between the nations of Guinea and Senegal dominated by the same French colonialism.
>
> (*Wretched*: 168–9)

In his essay 'Accra: Africa Affirms Its Unity and Defines Its Strategy', Fanon notes how men in Ghana, Ethiopia, Nigeria and Algeria have come together. Africans, he notes, 'pledged fidelity and assistance to one another', and 'no alliance will be rejected' (*African*: 157). It is this unity against a common colonial master that Fanon valorizes.

If Bankim in nineteenth-century India was projecting one culture/tradition – Hinduism – as the antidote to colonialism's cultures, Fanon posits a *commonality* of suffering and oppression that *all* Third World cultures experience. Cultural forms that address this commonality – and inspire rebellion – and champion the retrieval of older forms in folklore and oral traditions constitute 'combat literature' (*Wretched*: 173). These are the builders of a 'national literature' and a 'national consciousness', claims Fanon. However, Fanon is also clear that culture is inherently multiple and multi-layered: 'National culture is the sum of all these considerations, the outcome of tensions internal and external to society as a whole and its multiple layers' (177).

The retrieval of cultural practices works to counter the cultural threats posed by colonialism (Nayar 2008a: 97). We see several instances of this theme in anti-colonial and postcolonial writers. In Chinua Achebe's *Arrow of God* (1964) the local leaders 'hired a strong team of medicine-men to install a common deity for them. This deity which the fathers of the six villages made was called Ulu … ' (Achebe 1964: 17). The common deity becomes a focal point for the retrieval of tribal and collective memory and ritualized actions that would unite them. In Indian novelist Raja Rao's *Kanthapura* (1938) Rao uses Hindu mythology, the pastoral-agrarian setting of rural India, dialects and colloquialisms, and aligns these with an anti-colonial campaign at the Skeffington Coffee Estate. Rao's combination of myth with anti-colonial struggle is what makes the novel powerful, and is a good example of cultural nationalism in literature.

Interestingly, Fanon does not see cultural nationalism as concluding with independence. One cannot simply retrieve older cultural beliefs and systems and reinstall them as 'national culture', says Fanon. The retrieval of any culture must be based on the very beliefs and principles of the anti-colonial struggle: freedom from oppression, emancipation, equality, dignity and humanism. In a powerful passage Fanon writes: 'the future of culture and the richness of a national culture are also based on the values that inspired the struggle for freedom' (*Wretched*: 179). He thus rejects any unitary, singular 'culture' (179). This is Fanon's universal humanism at work, manifest as a deep suspicion of cultural nationalism which, he thinks, leads to xenophobia and genocide (borne out tragically in our time in Rwanda and other places). Fanon thus seeks a cultural formation beyond national boundaries. Vestiges of colonialism (especially in the form of new elites that inherit colonial modes of being) in a single African nation are a threat to African identity itself (180).

'On National Culture' carefully eschews identification with any tribe, ethnic group or nation in the African continent. Instead, Fanon calls for a larger stage, one where the tragedy of colonialism is staged by various actors across Africa. 'National culture' is the culture of this suffering, this legacy of colonialism, rather than any narrowly defined Algerian or Nigerian culture. Fanon is seeking, I suggest, a massive shift towards a whole state of the mutual recognition of suffering.

The rise and spread of such a national culture, Fanon argues, relies very often on the intellectuals in any society.

INTELLECTUALS, POETS AND PEASANTRY

In his essay 'On National Culture' (*Wretched*) Fanon acknowledged the role of intellectuals and the native bourgeois in reconstructing native pride, but was also emphatic that the peasantry and the working classes had a significant role to play in the process of decolonization. (Fanon was, however, uncertain as to the commitment of the working classes, see *African*: 64–72.)

THE INTELLECTUAL AND THE MASSES

Fanon sees the native intellectual or writer as moving through three stages (the terms are mine, not Fanon's):

- The Mimic Native: where he simply imitates his white master's culture.
- The Native in Transition: where he begins to move away from the white man's culture but has not fully returned to his own.
- The Decolonized Native: here the writer fully returns to his own culture and the masses, but can eventually move beyond immediate social contexts and racial identities.

As a mimic native the writer simply mimics the colonizer's culture and rejects his own, native one. The intellectual is overwhelmed by the colonizer's culture, is rootless and uncertain (experiencing 'vertigo', *Wretched*: 184). Fanon paints the picture of a thoroughly confused, 'split' intellectual, who sees hope only in the colonial's culture.

In the transition stage the writer's confidence in the white man's culture is shaken. However, he also cannot (re)turn to his native one because he has for some time now 'maintain[ed] an outsider's relationship to' his own people (*Wretched*: 159). The intellectual now begins to see virtues in the masses and in native cultures.

In the third stage the writer is finally agitated enough to 'rouse the people' (159). The alienation of the writer/intellectual's early life had produced only derivative work; once he returns to the people he begins to generate new ideas. This is the stage when the writers produce 'combat literature' and 'national literature'.

A truly national literature, Fanon argues, is combative (173). Fanon sees this literature as having an important role to play in shaping the future, 'open[ing] up new, unlimited horizons' (173). This work of 'opening up new, unlimited horizons' means:

1 the abandonment of those ideas and philosophies installed by the colonial master;
2 the solidarity of intellectuals/writers with the mass movement in the anti-colonial struggle so that they can abandon the colonial legacy and recognize the elitism that has estranged them from fellow-countrymen;
3 eventually reaching out beyond racial identities towards something larger and universal.

Fanon's sees intellectual 'work' as embedded in a social context: intellectual work is possible only when it is rooted in the *lived* experience of the colonized. Thus, Fanon criticizes those intellectuals and writers who speak expansively of Africa:

> The colonized intellectual, steeped in Western culture and set on proving the existence of his own culture, never does so in the name of Angola or Dahomey. The culture proclaimed is African culture.

> (*Wretched*: 150)

The writer feels that he must represent his *entire* race – a 'terrain' (Fanon's term) already given to him by the colonial master. Such writers are actually westernized intellectuals, alienated from their own cultures, a class of '*comprador* intelligentsia' (Appiah 1991), who have an ideological complicity with the west.

Fanon here is cautioning intellectuals against a shallow intellectualism, urging them instead to be embedded in actual social struggles. It cannot be, Fanon warns, that the intellectuals lead and the peasants will be 'led':

> The local party leaders must see to it that techniques seep into the desert of the citizen's brain so that the bridge in its entirety and in every detail can be integrated, redesigned, and reappropriated. In this way, and in this way only, everything is possible.

> (*Wretched*: 141)

Fanon here insists on local knowledge and cooperation: the masses must internalize ideas, the ideas cannot be imposed upon them (Lazarus 1993: 84).

Despite this embeddedness, Fanon wishes the intellectual to transcend racial polarities, and reach out for the universal (Posnock 1997). He might have to contradict the interests and ideas Algerians may have formed for themselves (Mowitt 1992). The intellectual therefore, functions as a 'split or disseminated character' (Mowitt 1992: 177). Fanon sees the decolonizing and postcolonial intellectual as one who can transcend the immediacy of social contexts and can be *self-reflexive* enough about the colonized itself. Fanon was aware of the necessity of historical awareness, especially of colonial exploitation, but he was also emphatic that the colonized cannot stay trapped in the past ('enclosed

in the materialized Tower of the Past' as he put it in *Black Skin*: 176).
Fanon was therefore against the whole 'back to roots' argument made
by anticolonials, and even postcolonials. (In, for example, the 1991
epic *Omeros*, Derek Walcott's Achilles walks back across the Atlantic to
his 'home', Africa, though Ngũgĩ's *Matigari*, 1989, represents such a
'homecoming' as a matter of crisis rather than celebration.)

Later commentators, while not explicitly referencing Fanon, point to
this urgent need for self-reflexivity among postcolonial intellectuals (see,
for example, Martinez 2003). Fanon himself, other commentators note,
was a postcolonial intellectual who would not stay circumscribed within
one tradition – either European or native (Forsdick and Murphy 2009;
Rajan 1997). When Fanon rejects a pure 'African' identity, and refuses
to be tied down to the mythical African past in *Black Skin*, he is
already moving towards his universalisms (of which more in Chapter 9
on humanism). Fanon's own engagement with a variety of European
thinkers (Marx, Freud, Lacan, Cesaire, Germaine Guex, Mannoni, Diop)
shows a complicated intellectual ancestry – which he deploys first as an
anti-colonial strategy and then as a self-reflexive, consciously universalist
mode of thinking. At no point, Fanon suggests, can we see the postcolonial intellectual as a nativist. It is this position, attitude and form of
thought in the postcolonialism that we need to take away from Fanon.

THE PEASANTRY, THE MASSES AND POLITICAL ORGANIZATION

Thus far we have seen Fanon's concern with the role of the intellectuals in
anti-colonial struggles and decolonization. We now turn to the second
component of any such struggle – the masses and their politicization.

The political mobilization of the masses involves, in Fanon's account:

- the role of the intellectual in consciousness-raising by going to the
  people;
- retrieving traditional cultural practices and beliefs to appeal to the
  masses and reduce the alienation of the intellectuals from the masses;
- revealing the collusion of the colonized elite with the imperial
  apparatus;
- showing how, in the postcolonial state, the new elites have occupied
  the same positions of power and exploitative authority as the
  former white masters.

Fanon treats political mobilization as the organization of traditional beliefs and institutions for the purpose of anti-colonial struggles and decolonization, where traditional institutions are reinforced and transformed and village assemblies become politicized.

Fanon recognizes the possible distance between the militant organizer – who is annoyed at the sight of the villagers going about their everyday lives without participating in political action (*Wretched*: 93) – and the masses. But, argues Fanon, the task of the intellectual and political activist is to 'nuance' the thinking of the masses (93). Once the masses have been roused, Fanon suggests, they will recognize the realities of colonialism. They will discover, for instance, that colonialism has actually empowered some natives: that 'some blacks can be whiter than the whites' (93). The task, Fanon notes, is to educate the masses to see how their own countrymen have colluded with the colonizers. (Fanon's views of the peasants as the true revolutionary class and his analyses of the class structures of African societies have been disputed, most notably by Jack Woddis, 1972. See also Caute, 1969.)

Such a mass consciousness-raising where such collusions are revealed, Fanon argues, has another interesting effect: it 'defuse[s] the overall hatred which the colonized feels toward the foreign settlers' (*Wretched*: 94). The colonist is no longer considered 'public enemy number one' (95) because some of the colonized have proved to be worse. The new political revolution, for Fanon, emerges from such a consciousness of imperialism and collusion, of mimicry and co-optation. Fanon might have overemphasized the role of a revolutionary peasantry, and is ambivalent about the role of radical intellectuals (McCulloch 1983: 153–4). In his 'The Africa to Come' Fanon is severe on the 'national middle classes' who, after independence, 'develop great appetites' (*African*: 186). As a result, notes Fanon, they become 'imperialist pseudo-states', the workers are oppressed in just the same way as they were in the colonial period, and trade unions and political parties become either ineffective or corrupt (186–7).

We see several postcolonial texts addressing this very point – the corruption of the postcolonial states, the failure to live up to the ideals of the freedom struggle, and the continuity between the white oppressor and the black/native 'heir' to the structures of power. In Rohinton Mistry's *A Fine Balance* (1995) we have a frightening insight into the functioning of a postcolonial state that has become the enemy of its people, as politicians and the petty bourgeois slip into the role vacated by the former white rulers.

THE CITY BELONGS TO YOU!
KEEP IT BEAUTIFUL!
FOOD FOR THE HUNGRY! HOMES FOR THE HOMELESS!
THE NATION IS ON THE MOVE!
                    (Mistry 1996: 373, emphasis in original)

The irony of these claims, issued by the state, is that the 'nation on the move' marginalizes its own citizens. Elites have taken over the government, the poor are displaced (the homeless are 'created' when their homes and hut-like tenements are cleared for 'progressive' urban structures and high-rises), and the helpless rendered vulnerable to exploitation as the nation 'moves'.

However, for such oppressed to rise in rebellion is not easy. Fanon admits that the landless, lumpen-proletariat have taken to drink and criminalism (*Wretched*: 81), but this is the consequence (his example is of Kenyans) of harsh colonial policies. The peasants lost their land (in Algeria) and became landless labourers. As modern farming technologies were introduced, traditional forms of agriculture disappeared, leaving the native peasant with little to do. The dispossessed peasant then moves to the city, but he remained poor and unemployed. Later, it is this class that takes to the revolution. Like the peasant, those employed in the industries, and workers such as taxi drivers, miners, dockers and nurses, lead miserable lives and are ready for a change, argues Fanon (*Wretched*: 64). They make up, writes Fanon, 'the most loyal clientele of the nationalist parties' (64). Indeed, Fanon sees militant action as a means through which the lumpen-proletariat – he lists prostitutes, vagrants and 'second-class citizens' (82) – becomes a revolutionary class. (Fanon is also aware of the easy corruptibility of the lumpen-proletariat, *Wretched*: 87.)

Fanon envisages a second revolution led by the lumpen-proletariat: the rebellion against the neo-colonial elite and the petty bourgeois that takes over power after independence. This is one of the less desirable consequences of nationalist consciousness, as we shall see in the next chapter.

SUMMARY

Fanon underscores the necessity of a 'black consciousness' and a pride in black culture (negritude) so that the colonized may acquire a sense of the Self as a *black human* Self. Colonialism has destroyed the black man's sense of self. Black consciousness is something that enables the colonized to transcend the psyche imposed on him and therefore to develop self-consciousness. Eventually, this self-consciousness and return to his own culture enables the black man to see his Self as connected to his *racial* identity. Black consciousness also frees the black from a relational identity where 'black' was always seen in relation to 'white'.

With such a black consciousness that enables a return to one's own culture, Fanon argues, we can see the rise of a national culture as well. National cultures, or cultural nationalism (of which negritude is one component), helps generate a sense of continuity with a community's past. It helps the colonized become alert to the malicious supplanting of their own culture by western culture. Cultural nationalism calls for and enacts a retrieval of those cultural practices that the colonial regime had sought to erase. But Fanon was also alert to the possible dangers of positing a unitary, or monolithic, national culture (of which more in the next chapter).

This consciousness-raising among the people demands the work of intellectuals, argues Fanon. He maps the growth of the intellectual-writer as passing through three stages. As a mimic native the writer simply mimics the colonizer's culture and rejects his own, native one, and is therefore alienated from his own culture. In the transition stage the writer's confidence in the white man's culture is shaken. He begins to see virtues in the masses and in native cultures. In the third stage the writer returns to the people and begins to generate new ideas, producing 'combat literature' and 'national literature'. The intellectual must be embedded in his native culture but, Fanon cautions, must eventual reach out beyond racial identities towards something larger and universal.

Turning to the role of the masses in anti-colonial struggles and decolonization, Fanon calls for a political mobilization of the masses. This requires, he argues, the intellectuals getting back in touch with the masses, the retrieval of traditional cultural practices and beliefs to appeal to the masses, and the awareness that the colonized elite had colluded with the imperialists. Decolonization necessitates the recognition that the new elites have occupied the same positions of power as the former white masters. This recognition might trigger a second revolution by the lumpen-proletariat where they rebel against the new brown/black elites.

8

NATIONALISM AND ITS PITFALLS

In the preceding chapter we saw how Fanon supported cultural nationalism and negritude as an essential component of (i) the anti-colonial struggle and (ii) the rising self-consciousness of the colonized. However, Fanon was also alert to the other, more painful, possibilities of cultural nationalism. In this chapter we turn to Fanon's critique of cultural nationalism and movements like negritude.

IN THE NAME OF THE NATION

While Fanon saw the need for cultural nationalism, negritude and self-consciousness for achieving a true decolonization, he was also aware of the possible consequences of such movements. Very often, for instance, nationalism becomes a weapon of exploitation by the neocolonial elites, where the exploitation is cloaked as 'national interest' (*Wretched*: 102). The neocolonial 'leaders' never stop being 'leaders' (127). This is a sentiment that postcolonial nations have all recognized: that after independence the white colonial master has been replaced by a dark-skinned one, all else – especially the exploitation – remaining the same.

We have already noted, towards the end of Chapter 7, Rohinton Mistry's critique of Indian 'development' that empowers the local elites but disempowers the already poor and deprived in postcolonial India. Like Mistry, numerous postcolonial authors have depicted the erosion of the ideals of the anti-colonial struggles, the descent into corruption and moral bankruptcy and the continued subjugation of the people by their own – i.e., native – masters.

We see in the fiction of Buchi Emecheta, Nigerian novelist Flora Nwapa (1931–93) and Kenyan-Canadian M. G. Vassanji (b. 1950), the corruption of the postcolonial societies of Africa. V. S. Naipaul attacks the philistinism and consumerism of Caribbean society. Tehmina Durrani (b. 1953) and Kamila Shamsie (b. 1973) map the religious bigotry and feudalism that continue to dominate Pakistani politics. Novelist Mistry, activist-novelist Arundhati Roy (b. 1961) and memoirs by the so-called lower castes (grouped as 'Dalits' in contemporary India) demonstrate how, despite political independence from white masters, structures of oppression have remained in place, albeit manned by brown masters in India. The elites, now as then, remain distant from their subjects. Their repeated use of the rhetoric of 'national good', as Mistry so superbly shows, often conceals deep social inequities, and the poor are sustainedly marginalized even in postcolonial nations.

Under such circumstances where the elites have failed to really enlighten the people and take the masses along, where a disconnect occurs between the rulers and ruled, there has been a return to ethnic tensions and tribalisms (*Wretched*: 105). Tribalisms were, of course, exactly the medication negritude's doctor ordered as a step towards decolonization. However, they soon lapse into xenophobia where every tribe turns against every other tribe, calls for the other's expulsion, and conditions lapse into xenophobia-driven genocide and ethnicide (105). In places like Sudan, the Congo, Somalia and Rwanda, ethnic strife has resulted in genocides and extreme suffering. The shift from anti-colonial cultural nationalism to xenophobic nationalism was something Fanon foresaw. This is where we need to acknowledge Fanon's prescience in his critique of negritude.

FANON'S CRITIQUE OF NEGRITUDE

Fanon's critique of negritude as a cultural and nationalist movement has various components that can be summarized as follows:

1   a rejection of negritude's idea of a single, homogenous black culture;
2   a rejection of negritude's theme of the purity of precolonial black culture, self-identical and complete;

3 a rejection of negritude's search for continuities with a precolonial era (negritude's concern with the past cultures of Africa;

4 a concern that negritude – with its overemphasis on culture – does not really alter the daily life of the black man in any significant way;

5 a refusal to see one's identity as formed *exclusively* by one's skin colour and culture (as negritude seems to suggest);

6 an impatience with negritude for privileging race over class in all cases.

Negritude, Fanon argued, cannot be based on a homogenous vision of black cultures. As he famously put it, 'there is not merely *one* Negro, there are *Negroes*' (*Black Skin*: 104, emphasis in original). With this, Fanon was calling for a multiplicity of interpretations of what 'black culture' itself meant. While he accepts that negritude has a definite role in the construction of an 'anti-colonial political consciousness' (Hanley 1976: 122), he also argues that this consciousness needs to go beyond homogenizing concepts.

Fanon has little patience with negritude's 'golden past', or what he terms a 'mystical past' ideal which ends up rejecting the present and the future of the nation (*Black Skin*: 7). While negritude contributes to the early moments of an anti-colonial consciousness it is when the colonized actually gets involved in the action against the colonizer that he begins to realize that he is primarily rooted in the local rather than in abstract and vague concepts like 'black culture'. He stops seeing the continent as a concept, and his meaning lies more in the national and the local, not in the mythical past but in the struggles of the present and, of course, the agenda for the future.

Criticizing thinkers like Césaire and Alioune Diop, Fanon argues that a valorization of the precolonial past is a mistake, it is to be 'enclosed in the materialized Tower of the Past' and become 'disalienated'. He does not want to be, states Fanon unequivocally, a 'man of any past', and would refuse to 'exalt' his past at the cost of his present and future (*Black Skin*: 176).

In his essay 'Racism and Culture', Fanon is harsh in his criticism of negritude (even though he does not mention the movement by name, it is implicit, I believe, in what he says):

> The customs, traditions, beliefs, formerly denied and passed over in silence are violently valorized and affirmed. Tradition is no longer scoffed at … The past,

becoming henceforth a constellation of values, becomes identified with the Truth.

(*African*: 42)

We see this Fanonian discomfort with the valorization of the past in other postcolonials as well. In Chapter 7 we saw examples of such valorization – in India's Tilak and the folkloric songs of the Mau Mau struggle, sometimes inventing new songs. Ngũgĩ wa Thiong'O's account of the song-and-dance routines of the struggle cited in the preceding chapter was pointing to the limitations of cultural nationalism and negritude's revivalisms. The past was not always a source of hope, they suggest. To move from decolonization to xenophobic cultural nationalism, Fanon and Ngũgĩ suggest, is *not* an option.

Instead of this invented past, Fanon argues for a different route to the new humanism he envisages for the formerly colonized:

I am a man, and what I have to recapture is the whole past of the world ... Every time a man has contributed to the victory of the dignity of the spirit, every time a man has said no to an attempt to subjugate his fellows, I have felt solidarity with his act.

(*Black Skin*: 176)

Such passages seem to indicate not only Fanon's 'disillusionment with negritude's celebration of an African past' but an 'identif[ication] with a larger history' (Bernasconi 2002: 73). However, it isn't a universal humanism either, in the conventional sense. What Fanon is expressing, especially in the passage immediately quoted above, is a solidarity with all those human beings who have fought subjugation.

Fanon also rejects negritude's idea that black perceptions of the world must be revived because they are unique. Fanon sees these as metaphysical speculations that do not in any way alter the white man's contempt or rejection of the black man and his culture. Fanon also does not see any 'purity' of African thought. In response to negritude's valorization of black values, he writes: 'It was not the black world that laid down my course of conduct. My black skin is not the wrapping of specific values' (*Black Skin*: 176). This is a clear repudiation of the authenticity argument: to have a particular skin colour is to possess authentic access to a culture or tradition. In a sense, this 'authenticity' of being black is what the colonial system also wants: each locked into the colour of the skin. As Fanon famously puts it: 'The white man is sealed in his whiteness. The black man in his blackness' (3). The colonial system can function only when 'types' and categories are put in place – and these require essentializing. The authenticity syndrome is the result of the colonial project of 'sealing' individuals into identities. Negritude, of course, seizes this same authenticity theme when it marks out the black man's humanity and difference from the colonial master. But, Fanon argues, merely emphasizing difference traps the black man in the continuing dialectic of black/white – a dialectic set in motion by the white man himself. While negritude might be a good point of departure in the making of a self-consciousness it is only a means to a larger, greater goal (humanism) and not an end in itself. Negritude simply reasserts, Fanon believes, the stereotype of primitivism installed by the colonial. Even negritude's rational argumentation did not find acceptance by the whites.

Thus Fanon notes how both the key modes of negritude – subscription to the stereotype of the irrational black and rational argumentation – were rejected by the whites. The colonial simply dismisses African society and its differences as an evolutionary 'stage of development' through which whites had *already* passed (*Black Skin*: 98). That is, blacks represented an early stage in human evolution through the ages, while white races represented later ('developed') stages.

The African is consigned to the 'primitive' stage of world history. More importantly, Fanon notes that emphasizing his 'blackness' (as negritude does) does not convince the colonial. In a moving passage he writes:

> Thus my unreason was countered with reason, my reason with 'real reason.' Every hand was a losing hand for me. I wanted to be typically Negro—it was no longer possible. I wanted to be white—that was a joke. And when I tried, on the level of ideas and intellectual activity, to reclaim my negritude, it was snatched away from me.
>
> (*Black Skin*: 101)

His 'irrational black' stereotype is greeted with implacable logic, his own logic rejected as illogical. What Fanon is arguing is: no negritude can survive in the diabolic context of colonial racism. As such, negritude, after developing a self-consciousness, has run its course.

Fanon here is rejecting the nativism that would emerge in numerous postcolonial nations whereby native, vernacular and local cultures would

be seen as pure, self-identical and 'natural' in the precolonial phase.
Fanon is gesturing at the messy nature of all culture, the borrowings,
the adaptations and the multiplicity of culture. He rejects the myth, in
other words, of cultural *purity* (a point, according to Gary Wilder,
2004, Césaire also makes): 'I secreted a race. And that race staggered
under the burden of a basic element. What was it? *Rhythm!*' (*Black
Skin*: 92–3). Fanon puts it in even harsher terms in his essay 'West
Indians and Africans': 'The truth is that there is nothing, *a priori*, to
warrant the assumption that such a thing as a Negro people exists ...
when someone talks to me about that "negro people", I try to
understand what is meant' (*African*: 18).

Fanon here rejects both the purity of a precolonial past and its
centrality to a new consciousness. He finds the idea of racial purity –
black or white – equally problematic. He argued that a category 'black
man' does not exist; neither does the 'white man'. Instead, in Fanon's
reading of racial identity, writes David Macey, 'black' and 'white' 'exist
only to the extent that they create one another in the course of the
sterile dialectic that pits a superiority complex against an inferiority
complex' (2004: 221). Both exist in relation to each other, but a
relation in which the white has the power of choice. The relationship
posited an essential 'good' white and a 'primitive' black one. To
therefore take recourse to such essentialisms (Fanon here is speaking
of negritude's essentializing of black identity) is to remain trapped in
the essentialisms that enabled colonial relations.

Racial identities come in useful for colonialism to structure relations
of power. Hence a return to catch-all categories such as 'the black
man' is to reinforce the very structural and identitarian conditions
that enabled the oppression of the African. Indeed, when Fanon
announces at the very beginning of *Black Skin* that his project is 'nothing
short of the liberation of the man of color from himself' (2), he is
speaking of a movement beyond fixed racial identities. This implies, I
argue, a movement *beyond colonial constructions of identities of blackness
but also transcends the essentialisms of negritude*.

Fanon argues that all precolonial cultures have been, to a greater or
lesser extent, modified – contaminated – by the culture of the colonizer.
Thus Fanon's rejection of negritude is not a rejection of its cultural
benefits but rather of its ideology of essentialism – which Fanon foresaw
as leading to a problematic identity politics. Fanon would prove to be
accurate in his prognosis as Rwanda, Sudan, Somalia and other African

nations descended into such a genocidal identity politics in the last decades of the twentieth century.

What Fanon is suggesting as justification for the rejection of negritude is that negritude homogenizes all black cultures and it does not prepare the blacks for dealing with the *future*. There is no universal 'African' or black experience, for Fanon. Further, any future for the blacks must begin by negotiating European civilization and European colonization of the blacks. Fanon's Marxism also causes him to argue that negritude's overwhelming emphasis on race results in an erasure of class. Thus, in the case of Martinique, Fanon suggests, 'a negro worker will be on the side of the mulatto worker against the middle-class Negro'. Fanon then underscores the economic basis of social identities: 'questions of race are but a superstructure, a mantle, an obscure ideological emanation concealing an economic reality' (*African*: 18). This is a crucial shift, for Fanon is proposing nothing less than an economic undermining of the cultural-political movement of negritude here. Any racial unification or antagonism, Fanon suggests, will be subordinated to class ideologies and solidarities, even among the blacks.

When he concludes *Black Skin*, Fanon visualizes a *deracinated* body, without colour: 'my final prayer: O my body, make of me always a man who questions' (181). This seems to gesture at once towards individualism and a universalism: of rationality, inquisitiveness and knowledge-seeking. This is a movement beyond negritude, which sought enlightenment and escape, identity and identification only within a hypothetical African tradition. When he declares: 'I made myself the poet of the world' (98), Fanon was seeking to escape a stereotype of the angry anti-colonial, opting instead for a prophet's role for the world's colonized and oppressed.

The 'poet of the world' also suggests a movement towards a universal humanism, and a retreat from the xenophobic cultural nationalisms of his time. The postcolonial who has attained a self-awareness through his anti-colonial struggle and decolonization needs to, in Fanon's view, reflect carefully on the legacies of negritude, the anti-colonial struggle and the risks of cultural nationalism. They should resist returning to essentialisms (the belief that cultures have a 'core' or 'essential' set of features). Instead they should be open to the world. It is from such a skepticism towards binaries and essential identities, whether national or racial, that an enlightened postcolonial might emerge, one who addresses the entire world.

This move toward a new humanism is perhaps Fanon's biggest legacy.

SUMMARY

Fanon saw the necessity of cultural nationalism, negritude and self-consciousness for achieving a true decolonization. Yet he was deeply troubled by the potential dangers inherent in emphasizing a cultural purity or singular identity. The neocolonial elites, he suspected, would become the new masters in the postcolonial society, and they would be as tyrannical and exploitative as the white masters – the only difference being that these would invoke 'national interest' as the driving force for xenophobia and oppression. Cultural nationalism, Fanon warns, could lapse into xenophobia where every tribe turns against every other tribe, calls for the other's expulsion, and conditions lapse into xenophobia-driven genocide and ethnicide, ostensibly in order to preserve national or cultural purity.

In his critique of negritude, Fanon first rejects the idea of a homogenous black culture, or a pure pre-colonial culture proposing instead a multiplicity of black cultures. One should not, warned Fanon, be trapped in nostalgia for a mythic past because myths do not change contemporary economic or social reality for the poor in the postcolonial nation. Finally, Fanon seeks to move beyond racial binaries and to speak on behalf of the world's sufferers, beyond geography and race. This move to transcend racial and national binaries is also a move towards formulating a new humanism.

9

A NEW HUMANISM?

The Negro is not. Any more than the white man. Both must turn their backs on the inhuman voices which were those of their respective ancestors in order that authentic communication be possible.

(*Black Skin*: 180)

Fanon's first major work, *Black Skin*, has a short Q&A section on its first page:

Why write this book? ...
Toward a new humanism ...
To understand and to love ...
(Black Skin: 1)

This 'new humanism', occurring in the pages of Fanon's oeuvre is not, and this is a point worth repeating, a return to the kind of humanism Europe has 'practised' since the Enlightenment.

This chapter suggests that Fanon's thought embodies a new humanism. It shows how Fanon's new humanism emerges in specific stages:

- Recognition is the foundation for self-consciousness. The formerly colonized who was never recognized by the white man, through the violent anti-colonial struggle has attained a self-awareness (a point made in preceding chapters).

- Ethical recognition accounts for and respects difference, and therefore recognizes the Other individual, culture, race.
- Ethical recognition generates an ethical commitment and responsibility to the lived experience of the Other, and is not interested in metaphysics or transcendent truths. This is a collective ethics.
- The collective ethics enable one to respond to the suffering of the Other, beyond racial, geographic and national boundaries or identities.
- This ability to respond to the suffering Other irrespective of racial or national identity is the foundation for a new humanism that is inclusive. The new humanism is solidarity with the world's oppressed.
- Such a response can emerge only from the formerly colonized who is able to move beyond national and racial boundaries.

THE 'PROBLEM' OF HUMANISM

European humanism spoke of a universal human and an essential humanity. This universal human had certain rights and fundamental qualities. However, blacks, Asians and women were excluded from the very category of 'human'. They were seen and treated as savages, beasts and sub-human. Two examples suffice to show how the universal category 'human' was not really universal: human came to mean white men. Rather than an inclusive category (which would mean all humans irrespective of race, gender or skin colour), humanism worked in practice as an exclusive one, leaving many out of the ambit of 'the human'.

African slavery, which originated in the fifteenth and sixteenth centuries when Europeans seized Africans and took them as labour to work on their plantations in the 'New World' of the Americas and the Caribbean, was justified on the grounds that the blacks were animals and therefore need not be treated as human. Humanism, thus conceived, was a doctrine that enabled colonialism and racial attitudes: once you have decided that the blacks were animals or savages then concepts like 'human rights' or 'human dignity' need not apply to them. They could be treated badly, like animals, because they were not human. Humanism thus, historically speaking, served the interests of powerful groups, especially Europeans.

Even when it promoted the cause of the poorer people of the world, this form of humanism was built around hierarchies of humanity. In England and Europe from the latter half of the eighteenth century the humanitarian regimes assumed that the poor, destitute, prostitutes, orphans, Africans and Asians were less than human. They were deemed to be inferior. But, instead of using this presumed hierarchy only for purposes of domination, the Europeans began to see it as an opportunity to perform noble acts. Humanitarianism emerged out of this sense of hierarchy: that since we (Europeans) are superior to other forms of human life, then it is our duty to improve their conditions, to look after them and be their protectors. This humanitarianism was a founding principle in the great 'civilizing mission' of the Europeans in their colonies, such as India. Once again, what emerges from this discussion is that humanism divided and ranked people on a scale where the European was at the top and all other races were at the bottom. In some cases this ranking of humans meant the 'lower' races would be dominated or eliminated, in other cases they would be 'improved' and 'reformed'. In both cases the word 'human' was attached only to the white races. Such a humanism that divides, ranks, dominates and excludes several ethnic and racial groups has to be fought.

Fanon is suspicious of such forms of humanism, and not of humanism in general. Thus he is able to acknowledge that 'all the elements of a solution to the great problems of humanity have, at different times, existed in European thought' (*Wretched*: 237). It is only within a racist system like colonialism that European humanism fails.

THE LIBERATED POSTCOLONIAL

Traditional European humanism fails because it accords no recognition to the black Other within colonialism, but demands that 'white' be recognized by the black. To achieve a 'reciprocal recognition' (as Fanon terms it) is to be *conscious* and alert to difference. Reflectivity, for Fanon, is central to the act of recognition. This reflectivity should be present in the formerly colonized, suggests Fanon, so that a transcendence of racial boundaries, which traditional humanism could not achieve, might be possible.

But what is the postcolonial like, after the struggle and decolonization? The composite picture that emerges from Fanon of this postcolonial would be as follows:

- the anti-colonial struggle gave the colonized a sense of the self;
- decolonization liberated this self from European frames of thought;
- national consciousness imbued a sense of local history and culture.

But now the formerly colonized needs to move beyond all this into a new plane of consciousness. He needs to free himself from both the racial dualisms (irrational, evil black *versus* rational, noble white) of colonialism as well as the essentialisms and binary identities of cultural nationalism. (There is, of course, a tension here. On the one hand, one wants to be recognized for being singular in ethnic or cultural identity, and would feel insulted if nobody enquired 'where are you from?' On the other, this question of particularity seems insulting because, apparently, it denies one's universality! See Hage 2010.)

The 'total liberation' of the formerly colonized is at once social and individual. Having recognized and fought colonial stereotypes and racial essentialisms, the postcolonial must reflect on racial identity but *not* be trapped by it – otherwise he simply repeats the colonial binaries of identity. This is precisely why Fanon expresses his unease with cultural nationalism (as we noted in Chapter 8).

Such a self-aware, reflective postcolonial consciousness will have 'a concept of man, a concept about the future of mankind' (*Wretched*: 143). Notice here that Fanon is *not* speaking about national or racial identity, but about mankind *in general*. This consciousness about 'the concept of man' and 'mankind' is the springboard for a new humanism. It begins with mutual recognition.

THE ETHICS OF RECOGNITION

For Fanon, violence is a means rather than an end. As we saw earlier, he sees the violence of the native as a consequence of the violence inherent in the colonial system itself. It helps the colonized to attain self-hood and it is the only language of colonial relations.

Fanon's question on the very first page of *Black Skin*, 'What does the black man want?' (1), is a question not about identity but *identification*. Fanon would answer this when he writes later in the book: 'I am asking to be considered' (170). Fanon argues that 'it is on recognition by that other being, that his own human worth and reality depend' (169). The black man and the white recognize and acknowledge each other. It is this reciprocity of recognition that is absent in colonial relations.

'Personhood' has been traditionally the privilege of the white man alone, and the black man is 'sealed into thingness', writes Fanon (*Black Skin*: 170), which suggests an absence of recognition and therefore a condition of dehumanization. 'He who is reluctant to recognize me opposes me', writes Fanon (170). Without this recognition there is no self-consciousness. Fanon suggests that the route to self-consciousness is via violence. When the white man, angered by the black man's violence and conflict, turns towards him and screams 'damn nigger' (172), the black man has finally managed to snatch a momentary *recognition*, albeit through a process of violence. Recognition, in other words, is the consequence of *struggle*.

This struggle is essentially a struggle by the colonized for his *humanity*: 'the former slave needs a challenge to his humanity' (*Black Skin*: 172). This is the trajectory one discerns in Fanon:

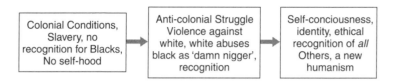

Colonial Conditions, Slavery, no recognition for Blacks, No self-hood → Anti-colonial Struggle Violence against white, white abuses black as 'damn nigger', recognition → Self-conciousness, identity, ethical recognition of *all* Others, a new humanism

The black has fought for and gained recognition *as a black man*. His humanity has been finally recognized. It is this *ethical* recognition of the particularity of the black man that leads to decolonization, of both the black and the white. In 'Racism and Culture' Fanon spoke of the 'universality [that] resides in this decision to recognise and accept the reciprocal relativism of different cultures, once the colonial status is irreversibly excluded' (*African*: 44). This ethical recognition of difference, of individuals, races and cultures, is the basis of a new humanism because it encompasses the globe.

Fanon, however, is careful to insist that recognition cannot be restricted to the intellectual and cultural domains. His critique of negritude foregrounds this view that cultural recognition does not change colonial material realities:

> it would be of the greatest interest to be able to have contact with a Negro literature or architecture of the third century before Christ. I should be very happy to know that a correspondence had flourished between some Negro philosopher and Plato. But I can absolutely not see how this fact would change anything in the lives of the eight-year-old children who labor in the cane fields of Martinique or Guadeloupe.
>
> (*Black Skin*: 180)

Recognition is the acknowledgement of cultural and historical realities of other *humans*. True decolonization depends upon both, whites and blacks, colonizers and colonized, seeing and respecting difference. In his 'Racism and Culture' Fanon spells out his vision for this ethics of recognition and difference:

> The occupant's spasmed and rigid culture, now liberated opens at last to the culture of the people who have never really become brothers. The two cultures can affront each other, enrich each other. In conclusion, universality resides in this decision to recognise and accept the reciprocal relativism of different cultures, once the colonial status is irreversibly excluded.
>
> (*African*: 44)

It is significant that Fanon speaks of a *mutual* enrichment. For those who see Fanon as exclusionary and committed to violence, this argument ought to function as a corrective. Anticolonial violence has resulted in (i) the whites' acknowledgement of the black, (ii) the black discovering a Self, (iii) an acknowledgement of mutual difference (between blacks in Africa as well as blacks from whites). From this point onwards, decolonization proceeds through this process of mutual recognition of cultures, cultural difference and mutual trans-formation. Fanon underscores the possibility of mutual enrichment as a consequence of the ethics of recognition. What he is arguing for is that once the unequal power relations of colonialism have been excluded, decolonization can lead to the *mutual transformation of the colonizer and the colonized.*

Fanon seeks nothing less than the complete overthrow of a humanism based on exclusion and traditional categorizations. In its place he seeks a humanism where difference is respected. Humanism in Fanon is the result of this 'reciprocal relativism of different cultures' where the black is no mere 'object' but a black human for the white. In similar fashion the white is not just the white oppressor/master but a white human. This humanism is not about emulating the model of human embodied in the European, who is, as Fanon points out, part of a race of 'murderers' (*Wretched*: 236), but to accept the black man *as a human in his own right*. The human cannot, Fanon suggests, be defined (as classical humanism has done since the Enlightenment) only in comparison to the European model of the 'human'. The African (and, by extension, women, Asians and members of any racial group) must be a human in and of himself, and not evaluated from the European perspective.

Ethical recognition entails:

- recognizing the identity, personhood and cultural identity of all *Others;*
- a *mutuality* of recognition;
- respecting *difference* but neither erasing/homogenizing nor penalizing difference.

The violence of the colonized, as we have already noted, enables a self-realization in Fanon's scheme of things. Once this self-realization occurs in the formerly colonized, we can see a progress towards a collective self-realization that promotes a more inclusive humanism. Gerald Tucker suggests that in Fanon the violence of the colonized promotes a 'true spirit of community' whereas colonial violence 'prohibits the sharing of community feelings' (1978: 408). The emergence of this sense of the collective, and collective ethics, in Fanon is our next concern.

COLLECTIVE ETHICS

With the recognition of difference comes a recognition of the collective Other as well. However, Fanon is also emphatic that the recognition of the collective entails a collective responsibility. After decolonization, the task of nation-building must be based on socialism and equality, argues Fanon. Social and political responsibility must accompany power and wealth.

Fanon sees political independence as a limited goal, a stage in the greater journey towards humanism. Fanon argues that the individual and the citizen both need to evolve because:

> Independence has certainly brought the colonized peoples moral reparation and recognized their dignity. But they have not yet had time to elaborate a society or build and ascertain values.
>
> (*Wretched*: 40)

Fanon is proposing a socially committed individual citizen who emerges in the wake of decolonization. It was in the course of the anti-colonial struggle that the colonized attained a sense of the Self. But once the anti-colonial struggle is over and the process of decolonization underway then the newly discovered self-consciousness must become concerned about *more* than the Self.

Fanon urges leaders of new states to focus on economic and social building. He calls for a shift from the earlier struggle: where once the natives fought the colonizer, they must now fight 'poverty, illiteracy, and underdevelopment' (*Wretched*: 51). Fanon argues that the leaders in the postcolonial context have adopted a 'policy of neutrality' (40). The difficulty, as Fanon sees it, is to balance the political and cultural independence of the new nation-state while at the same time seeking economic aid from foreign nations (who, of course, seek to impose economic and trade policies that suit their capitalist interests). Fanon points out that depending on a foreign country (preferably socialist) is not out of the question, because Europe itself had been built on the 'the sweat and corpses of blacks, Arabs, Indians, and Asians' (53). A collective ethics, for Fanon, is primarily economic: the equitable distribution of resources, wealth and labour. Pointing to colonialism as marked by a fundamental asymmetry of resource distribution, Fanon writes: 'what matters today … is the need for a redistribution of wealth' (55).

Fanon's emphasis on socialism means he prefers the collective ethics of the new nation rather than the individualist ethics of the west (Jean-Marie 2007: 14). This new socialism-determined humanism is oriented towards *action and lived experience* rather than abstract or metaphysical transcendence. (One of Fanon's early commentators, Gerald Tucker, 1978, noted this emphasis on action as ethics in Fanon.)

In a valuable commentary Richard Pithouse (2003) has proposed that Fanon rejected abstract theorizing that was not connected with the lived realities of people. Fanon famously wrote that the aim of philosophy and theory must be to 'educate man to be actional' (*Black Skin*: 173). The working, unemployed and starving natives, wrote Fanon, 'do not say they represent the truth because they are the truth in their very being' (*Wretched*: 13). He rejects, also, cultural atavism and reactionary returns to the mythic 'glorious' past (as we saw in his critique of negritude). Fanon writes about this quest for a cultural heritage that ignores contemporary reality where 'the actual existence of an Aztec civilization has done little to change the diet of today's Mexican peasant' (148). What Fanon seeks is praxis for a collective development. He rejects intellectual work that produces myths that do not solve the newly independent nation's problems.

Humanism born out of such a praxis seeks nothing less than the amelioration of the sufferings of people in the present rather than transcendent truths about history. This humanism is a collective ethics that is pragmatic rather than idealist. It is rooted in the present history, local and specific. Fanon's insistence on the 'actional' and his rejection of empty intellectualism turns away from European models (of transcendent human history) as well as the glorification of one's own past.

BEYOND NATIONAL CONSCIOUSNESS, TOWARDS UNIVERSALISM

Fanon opens *Black Skin* with some interesting declarations: 'Mankind, I believe in you' (1) and 'I believe that the individual should tend to take on the universality inherent in the human condition' (3). It is significant that Fanon, for all his rootedness in Algeria and Africa, is emphatic about the need to address universals. He calls upon the formerly colonized to recognize, in the words of one critic, both 'concrete persons and abstract collectives' (Bamyeh 2010: 53).

This universalism stems from a particular humanist component of his thought. In what follows I want to draw out the implications of Fanonian thought for a new humanism.

Fanon's humanism may be summarized as follows:

- He sees processes like colonialism as dehumanizing *both* the black and the white, and thus sees both as victims to the condition.
- Underneath the tyrannical colonizer and the black victim are human beings, suggests Fanon.
- He argues that we should evaluate humans by their actions rather than their racial, ethnic or national identities.
- The formerly colonized emerges from the colonial condition self-aware and a new human who can transcend national boundaries.
- This new human, the formerly colonized, responds to the suffering of the world, building solidarities with other sufferers.

Fanon, in other words, *entrusts the task and the project of a more inclusive humanism to the formerly colonized*, i.e., the 'Third World'. This is a major shift from European humanism.

Fanon's humanism is solidarity with the *world*'s suffering, irrespective of race, colour or geography. He writes:

> The new relations are not the result of one barbarism replacing another barbarism, of one crushing of man replacing another crushing of man. What we Algerians want is to discover the man behind the colonizer; this man who is both the organizer and the victim of a system that has choked him and reduced him to silence.
>
> *(Dying*: 32)

This is an amazing observation. Fanon has aligned the colonizing white man with the colonized black, both as victims of a cruel process. Fanon's work, I believe, is about the *world's oppressed*, and when he includes the white man as a victim of colonialism he has sought to move beyond the racial binary. Suffering and oppression are unifying factors for his thoughts about humanism – and these factors enable him to call for a consciousness beyond nationalisms. In another essay, 'Letter to the Youth of Africa', Fanon writes:

> It is essential that the oppressed peoples join up with the peoples who are already sovereign if a humanism that can be considered valid is to be built to the dimensions of the universe.
>
> *(African*: 114)

Fanon is speaking of an alignment between races. 'If the color black is virtuous, I shall be all the more virtuous the blacker I am' (*African*: 23). With this savagely ironic comment, Fanon proceeds to reject the myth of authenticity, which he describes as 'the great black mirage' (27). Ross Posnock argues that Fanon's rejection of such racial binaries and essentialisms enables him to move beyond identity to *action* (Posnock 1997: 339). This 'action', as Posnock sees it, is intellectual work. This intellectual work in the decolonizing phase is essentially, in Fanon, a turn away from the traditional national liberation politics towards an internationalism and universalism (what Nigel Gibson identifies as the third mode of nationalism in Fanon: Gibson 2003, chapter 8). This internationalism is based on human action rather than a blind adherence to national identities. Fanon, therefore, calls for consciousness beyond the national.

This self-awareness of the limitations of nationalism and national cultures, argues Fanon, 'guarantees' greater communication. In an important comment, Fanon says: 'National consciousness, which is not nationalism, is alone capable of giving us an international dimension' (*Wretched*: 179). Fanon therefore speaks of 'universalizing values' (180) as a counter to nationalism. What Fanon is proposing is that revolutionary movements might be national and nationalist to begin with, but the consciousness they engender must enable a movement *beyond* the national towards the universal. For this the individual must become self-aware, and this self-awareness is the route to his own liberation (this self-awareness of the formerly colonized Africans, or for that matter Asians, unfortunately, has not happened: see Lazarus 1994: 200). Once the individual has been fully liberated through (i) revolutionary struggle, and (ii) national culture and consciousness, *he is ready to free himself of both colonialism and nationalism and become a new man*. This new man is social, seeks the universal and recognizes the Other. This postcolonial in Fanon is possessed of a greater 'intellectual sensitivity', as one commentator termed it (Bamyeh 2010: 60). In what is arguably a manifesto for the new humanist postcolonial, Fanon writes:

Since the individual experience is national, since it is a link in the national chain, it ceases to be individual, narrow and limited in scope, and can lead to the truth of the nation and the world.

(*Wretched*: 140–1)

As the individual strives to free his nation, he also 'will[s] here and now the triumph of man in his totality' (*Wretched*: 141). Any great revolutionary struggle, for Fanon, will lead to a consciousness that ushers in a new human: 'this new humanism is written into the objectives and methods of the struggle' (178). With social and political liberation comes the liberation of the self for both colonizer and colonized, and this is the starting point for the new human. The formerly colonized therefore, in order to free himself in totality, 'brings all his resources into play, all his acquisitions, the old and the new, his own and those of the occupant' (*African*: 43). He recognizes, appropriates and internalizes the Other in order to transcend both, his and the white man's identities. Thus the anti-colonial struggle and its political experience is the source of a new humanism because it facilitates the rise of a new consciousness.

The *self-determined, self-aware liberated postcolonial individual therefore is at the core of Fanon's new humanism*. This individual is able to engage in the reciprocal recognition which leads to the new humanism. Such a reciprocal recognition is achieved through the recognition of shared suffering. Further, such an individual is able to reflect on the potential for anti-humanist xenophobia. Humanism in Fanon begins when he asks for dismantling *not only the racial binaries of colonialism but also the xenophobic cultural nationalism of postcolonial nations.*

Such a dismantling is possible only when one moves beyond the racial binaries of colonialism and the xenophobia of cultural nationalism, forging instead a relation with the *world*'s suffering. This is yet another strand to Fanon's universalist humanism. Building solidarities on the basis of a shared history of suffering – no matter what your racial–ethnic–national identity might be – is the new humanism that Fanon seeks.

Albert Memmi was one of the first to point out that Fanon 'gradually identified his own destiny with Algeria, then with the Third World, and ultimately with all of humanity' (1973: 33). Memmi was one of the first to point to Fanon's *centrifugal* model of humanism, moving outward from individual to community to ethnic group to nation to the race and then, finally, the world.

Fanon's humanism anticipates the work of several postcolonial theorists, notably that of Leela Gandhi (2006) and Ashis Nandy (1987, 1998). Gandhi notes the affective communities built during colonialism where a commonality of interests – from vegetarianism to spirituality – brought the whites and the Indians together. Nandy's is a far more Fanonian move. In two major essays, 'Towards a Third World Utopia' (1987) and 'A New Cosmopolitanism: Toward a Dialogue of Asian Civilizations' (1998), Nandy calls for a new solidarity of peoples, one based on a shared culture of suffering. Nandy writes:

> The only way the Third World can transcend the sloganeering of its well-wishers is, first, by becoming a collective representation of the victims of man-made suffering everywhere in the world and in all past times, second, by internalizing or owning up the outside forces of oppression and, then, coping with them as inner vectors and third by recognizing the oppressed or marginalized selves of the First and Second Worlds as civilizational allies in the battle against institutionalized suffering.

(2004 [1987]: 441)

This is Nandy's reasoning: 'If the Third World's vision of the future is handicapped by its experience of man-made suffering, the First World's future, too, is shaped by the same record' (467). Sidi Omar argues that Fanon seeks to 'initiat[e] a new history for humankind in which the Third World is to be entrusted with a leading role' (2009: 272), an argument that echoes Nandy. I have argued elsewhere that a shared history of trauma and suffering can offer an 'affective cosmopolitanism' (Nayar 2008b). In Nandy's case, I argued, this sense of shared suffering might be a different way of thinking about future humanity. Nandy writes:

> Ultimately it is not a matter of synthesizing or aggregating different civilizational visions of the future. Rather, it is a matter of admitting that while each civilization must find its own authentic vision of the future and its own authenticity in future, neither is conceivable without admitting the experience of co-suffering which has not brought some of the major civilizations of the world close to each other.
>
> (Nandy 1987: 468)

Both Nandy and Fanon point to the response to suffering as being at the core of a new humanism. Fanon's call has two components:

1 With his call to move beyond the dualism of racial identity and colonialism, Fanon opts out of racial identities itself.
2 By arguing that the colonizer is both 'organizer and the victim of a system that has choked him and reduced him to silence', he aligns the perpetrator with the victim (colonized) in a continuum of suffering. Decolonization would lead to the freedom of both colonizer and colonized from this victimhood. It is in the recognition of mutual suffering that a new humanism can emerge.

To this end, Fanon suggests, even nationalism must turn to universalism: 'If nationalism is not explained, enriched, and deepened, if it does not very quickly turn into a social and political consciousness, into humanism, then it leads to a dead-end' (*Wretched*: 144). To suffer with the world's wretched – this is the humanism that Fanon proclaims when he quotes Césaire: 'There is not in the world one single poor lynched bastard, one poor tortured man, in whom I am not also murdered and humiliated' (45). Thus Fanon writes of the shared history of colonialism which might, if recognized, lead to a new humanism on the part of the formerly colonized nations:

> There is no common destiny between the national cultures of Guinea and Senegal, but there is a common destiny between the nations of Guinea and Senegal dominated by the same French colonialism.
>
> (*Wretched*: 168–9)

The new human claims the '"right to citizenship" in a world of "reciprocal recognitions"' (Azar 1999: 31), and is the foundation for a 'transnational humanism' (Alessandrini 1998). What contemporary commentators such as Alessandrini, Azar and Ahluwalia (2003) see in Fanon is the necessity (and possibility) of moving outwards from Algeria as a specific instance of racial exploitation that denies humanity, to the world at large, in a transnational history of oppression. We see numerous occasions where Fanon called for a humanism that originated in the Algerian Revolution but then moves beyond it to encompass the world, and all those places and peoples that experience oppression. Take, for instance, the last sentences of three of his works: 'This oxygen,' writes Fanon, 'which creates and shapes a new humanity – this, too, is the Algerian Revolution' (*Dying*: 160). And in *African*: 'The liberation of the Algerian national territory is a defeat for racism and for the exploitation of *man*; it inaugurates the unconditional reign of justice' (64, emphasis added). And the final sentence of *Wretched* reads: 'For Europe, for ourselves and for humanity, comrades, we must make a new start, develop a new way of thinking, and endeavor to create a new man' (239). Fanon clearly sees the Africans as acting in solidarity with the 'underdeveloped peoples' (143). In each case Fanon moves beyond Martinique, Algeria and Africa to include the colonized world itself. While David Macey is correct in reading Fanon as a Martinician theorist of Algerian colonization (2000: 26–30), there is a strong case to be made, based even on the selective quotations above, for arguing for a Fanon embedded in Algeria but looking at the world beyond, a humanist rooted in the immediate anti-colonial struggle of Algerians, but expressing solidarity with the rest of the colonized people.

Fanon's humanism, I suggest, must be treated as *potential* rather than actual. His books end with prayers, promises and hopes – all of which are about the future. His references to the humanity 'to come' are indices of the *potential* for a new humanity. Fanon constantly underscores work, action and vision, all of which must be future-directed (something we see in the work of Paul Gilroy, 2000, as well).

The argument about a new humanism is best summarized in Fanon's own words:

> Every time a man has contributed to the victory of the dignity of the spirit, every time a man has said no to an attempt to subjugate his fellows, I have felt solidarity with his act.
>
> (*Black Skin*: 176)

SUMMARY

Fanon's humanism emerges through a very specific set of arguments. In his work on violence he suggests that colonialism denies recognition and therefore identity to the colonized. It is on the principle of recognition that all identity rests. Once the native has discovered his Self through the anti-colonial struggle, he becomes more self-aware. A proper and fuller decolonization is possible when the colonized frees himself from the binaries of racial identities established by the colonial apparatus.

Ethical recognition that results from a decolonized mind-set accounts for and respects difference, and therefore recognizes the Other individual, culture and race. It generates an ethical commitment and responsibility to the lived experience of the Other, and is not interested in metaphysics or transcendent truths. This is a collective ethics which enables one to respond to the suffering of the Other, beyond racial, geographic and national boundaries or identities. Such a collective ethics calls for a response to suffering – anybody's suffering. Such an ability to respond to the suffering Other irrespective of racial or national identity is the foundation for a new humanism that is inclusive. The new humanism is solidarity with the world's oppressed.

Finally, Fanon suggests that this ethical response can emerge only from the formerly colonized who is able to move beyond national and racial boundaries. This chapter has demonstrated a significant overlap between Fanon's humanism and other postcolonial theorists who, like Fanon, also speak of universalisms of suffering. It is also important to note that all of them speak of the 'Third World' as being at the forefront of the campaign against suffering – a point Fanon made so forcefully in *Black Skin* by expressing solidarity with anybody who battles oppression.

AFTER FANON

Fanon's influence and legacy can be seen in diverse disciplines. Essays and books with titles such as 'remembering Fanon' and 'rethinking Fanon' indicate his continued influence on twentieth-century thought. From Fanon's oeuvre the following ideas have circulated, often in tangential or fragmented forms, within postcolonial theory, literary and cultural studies, philosophy and political theory:

- the struggle for retrieving subjugated knowledges;
- constructing a more inclusive humanism free of the colonial legacy while retaining the secular humanism of the Enlightenment;
- the necessity of a self-reflexive postcoloniality;
- the need to retain in the postcolonial state the emancipatory ideologies that drove the anti-colonial struggle;
- the disavowal of the dualisms and essentialisms of the colonial past;
- the refusal to idealize a past by ignoring the present and future.

There is no one Fanon. Fanon has been appropriated by thinkers of different philosophical and theoretical persuasions. Thus we have the poststructuralist Fanon in Homi Bhabha, where, especially in his Forewords to new editions of Fanon, Bhabha emphasizes hybridity, ambivalence and ruptures in Fanon's thought. Seeking to demonstrate a fracture within colonial discourse, Bhabha positions Fanon as somebody who recognized this fracture as well. Sekyi-Otu claims him as a philosopher of political experience. Anthony Alessandrini, an astute Fanon commentator, captures these multiple modes of claiming Fanon's legacies when he writes of Fanon's 'multiple themes, voices, and methodologies' being claimed by many (2005: 434). In anthropology, scholars like Udo Krautwurst (2003) have used Fanonian frameworks to read colonial conditions such as settler colonialism. Fanon's significant influence on contemporary African and Caribbean literature and philosophy, most notably that of Edouard Glissant, has also come in for sustained attention (see Mardorossian 2009). Hussein Adam (1993) has argued persuasively that we should see Fanon as a democratic theorist. Adam reads Fanon as making a strong case for self-determination, but refuses to accept any collective self-determination that does not ensure individual agency and freedom. Fanon's appropriation has seen interesting trajectories (and found its share of critics, notably Gates and Gibson) in literary and cultural studies in both Britain and the USA. Prior to this there was the African appropriation of Fanon in the 1960s and the Black Panther movement's Fanonism of the 1960s and 1970s in the USA. Steve Biko in South Africa was an ardent Fanonist and found Fanon useful for his black consciousness movement in the 1970s. From the late 1980s and early 1990s, the rise of cultural studies as a disciplinary formation and the concomitant rise of postcolonial studies saw an interesting alignment. Homi Bhabha's work on Fanon was enthusiastically received by the British cultural studies scholars, notably Stuart Hall (1996). Black British artists have worked with Fanonian ideas as well (embodied in a critical study, *Facts of Blackness: Frantz Fanon and Visual Representation*, 1996). Numerous novelists and writers also exhibit Fanonian tendencies, as we shall see.

What I focus on in this chapter on 'After Fanon' is a selective examination of interesting appropriations and re-readings of Fanon's oeuvre, primarily within postcolonial studies.

FANON, RESISTANCE AND BLACK CONSCIOUSNESS

Fanon's cautious support of negritude and the black consciousness idea was influential among the anti-apartheid campaigns of the 1970s in South Africa. Later postcolonial scholars have suggested that Fanon might have been influential in the kind of cultural politics that evolved as part of these campaigns (Ahluwalia and Zegeye 2001). Such work excavates Fanonian influences in resistance movements in order to show how he has been appropriated and extended.

Steve Biko, one of the prominent leaders of the South African anti-apartheid movement, campaigned for a 'black consciousness', pride in their values and ways of life, as a way of decolonizing themselves. The campaign was clearly directed at a rethinking of European models of modernity. Ahluwalia and Zegeye suggest that Biko's and the urban black's critique of European modernity was Fanonian because they were questioning the cultural politics of colonial ethnography, sociology and anthropology, which consistently portrayed – to the blacks in schools as well – the supposed inferiority of black races and culture (Ahluwalia and Zegeye 2001: 464–5). Biko's insistence on a return to black culture as a mode of resistance, in this reading, echoes Fanon's arguments about decolonization as a cultural process.

Fanon has been appropriated as a theorist of anti-colonial resistance because he refuses to accord a totality to colonial power. In this scheme of extending Fanon, critics like Homi Bhabha and Benita Parry treat Fanon as embodying ambivalence and ruptures (Bhabha 2008; Parry 1987. This interpretation has attracted criticism from JanMohamed 1985 and Gates 1991).

FANON, NATIONALISM, INTERNATIONALISM

Fanon was emphatic that any nationalism that does not move towards internationalism was unacceptable. He saw nationalism as a starting point for the building of a new consciousness, subjectivity and humanism which would abandon the European Enlightenment's colonialism-tinged one and substitute it with a more inclusive humanism. Fanon's critique of both colonialism and anti-colonial/nationalist thought has found resonance in the postcolonial thought of the late 1990s. That is, I see Fanon's emphasis on the inherent dangers of nationalism as visible in particular modes of postcolonial critique that:

1 reject traditional binaries of imperial complicity versus nationalism;
2 emphasize hybridity and ambivalence;
3 detect 'internal' (that is European) forms of anti-colonialism that align themselves with native (non-European) anti-colonial thought in a kind of *internationalism*.

While making a move from Fanonian suspicion of nationalism to a (new) postcolonial rewriting of internationalism and globalism might seem far-fetched, I believe that Fanon's humanism did encompass such a vision. Take, for instance, Fanon's vision of Marxism. Fanon proposed that 'Marxist analysis should always be slightly stretched every time we have to do with the colonial problem' (*Wretched*: 5). This 'stretch' could be interpreted to mean a greater inclusivity, where Fanon was proposing an international socialism that would account for the legacy of colonialism and would not exclude women, the blacks and other races/groups. This inclusivity is a more nuanced analysis of both the colonial and postcolonial condition, for Fanon refused to work within the old binaries of white versus black, empowered versus dis-empowered. He refused to codify theoretical frames and interpretive scaffolding ('stretch', Fanon says) so that the frame did not become a new norm, dogma or fashion. In recent work in postcolonial studies Fanon's legacy has figured in interesting ways, most notably in this 'stretch', or the movement beyond essential binaries and the quest for a more inclusive humanism (even within the colonial condition).

Leela Gandhi's seminal *Affective Communities* (2006) is not a 'Fanon' book (indeed, Fanon does not find any mention here). But her focus on forms of nationalism in India that had *emotional* resonances for particular varieties of anti-imperialists in England suggests the existence, in the late nineteenth and early twentieth century, of a sub-species of humanism that was internationalist. To argue that such forms of alliances between Indians and Englishmen and women undergirded by a belief in vegetarianism or mysticism constituted a form of political resistance through interracial friendship is, I suggest, to argue for a new humanism that Fanon gestured at towards the end of *Wretched*: 'a new start, develop a new way of thinking, and endeavor to create a new man' (239). Gandhi argues a case for paying attention to the 'aspirational energy' of:

> Colonial actors ... [who] might have performed their political vocation impa-tiently from within imperial culture, unwilling to wait for its eventual hybridiza-tion, actively renouncing, refusing, and rejecting categorically its aggressive manicheanism.
>
> (Gandhi 2006: 5)

In the nineteenth century, Gandhi demonstrates, numerous European mystics found intellectual companionship with Indians, and thus constituted a hybridized, internationalist 'community'. This, she proposes, was a political alliance, even though the community's focus or interests would be strictly classifiable as the 'political'. Here national cultures and cultural nationalism that produced one form of subjectivity and humanism (in the European Enlightenment) is abandoned in favour of a more inclusive humanism and community-linkage that defies the traditional frames of the 'colonial' as well as the 'political'.

From Gandhi's reading of the mystics of nineteenth-century colonial India and imperial Britain, we see how the alliance of mystics became a political community that did not fit into the colonial structure but envisaged a new internationalist humanism. We see in Gandhi's analysis the loci of a Fanonian internationalism that draws upon national cultural practices but are clearly *not* constrained by them.

FANON, CULTURAL IDENTITY, DECOLONIZATION

We have already noted Fanon's criticism of the mimicry of the colonizer by the colonized in preceding chapters. A decolonization of the mind, Fanon insisted, was mandatory for the colonized to be truly and completely free of the colonial. This might require a return to one's cultural practices so that the colonial's practices may be abandoned.

'I had no nation now but the imagination', wrote the Caribbean poet Derek Walcott ('The Schooner *Flight*'), and perhaps this is a Fanonian stance. We see this Fanonian emphasis on imagination, intellectualism and decolonization in numerous postcolonial writers. (C. L. Innes notes Fanonian influences in the Kenyan Ngugi, Walcott, Nigerian Achebe and Caribbean George Lamming, 2007: 12–13.) Michelle Cliff discovers her Jamaican roots and displaces the 'King's English' and Gloria Anzaldúa displaces Spanish when she mixes Spanish, English and Nahuatl. Linguistic acrobatics in Achebe, Rushdie and Kincaid, narrative experiments with forms of storytelling in which western modes of storytelling are undermined by the use of native ones – the best example would be Rushdie's *Midnight's Children* where Rushdie uses the Arabian Nights and the Arab-Islamic forms of narrative such as the *kissa* and the *dastaan* alongside the western novel's linear narrative and the Hindu *kahani* – are not merely acts of linguistic rebellion against a colonial legacy. They are modes of 'decolonizing the mind' through acts of imagination and enunciation.

> Imaginary constructions go hand in hand with *enunciations*, and loci of enunciations are unthinkable without a language ... Insofar as loci of enunciation are territorial, in the conditions of both their possibilities and their performances, Fanon, Cliff, and Anzaldúa all enact a displacement of the understanding subject ... relocated at the limits ... of the Western tradition and colonial expansion.
>
> (Mignolo 2005: 193, emphasis in original)

Mignolo here underscores the *politics of imagining differently*, where acts of imagination are inseparable from acts of enunciation, and enunciation itself is social. If this is the case then major claims might be made for literature and imaginative works as social instruments that revitalize the (social, collective) imagination. This too is a Fanonian legacy. Fanon defined national culture as the 'collective thought process' of a people (*Wretched*: 168), where a transformative 'collective thought process' implies an education of the masses through *cultural expressions*: poetry and artisanship. Fanon himself began with the poetry of Aimé Césaire. From imagining alternate worlds to enunciating them as part of a 'collective thought process' is the postcolonial challenge.

Novelists like Chinua Achebe, Tsitsi Dangarembga and Jackie Huggins have in their fiction foregrounded the loss of native history and underscored the need to retrieve and replenish the colonial histories with their own. 'Their history. Fucking liars. Their bloody lies. They've trapped us. They've trapped us', screams Nyasha in Dangarembga's *Nervous Conditions* (1988: 201). In Ama Ata Aidoo's *Our Sister Killjoy* she writes:

> A common heritage. A
> Dubious bargain that left us
> Plundered of
> Our gold
> Our tongue
> Our life – while our
> Dead fingers clutch
> English – a
> Doubtful weapon fashioned
> Elsewhere to give might to a
> Soul that is already fled.
>> (Aidoo 1977: 28–9)

The language, the histories, the forms of narration have all disenfranchised the colonized and alienated him from his roots. The process of decolonization involves (i) recognizing the 'traps' of colonial history and (ii) finding a way of rewriting, reclaiming, native histories. In Walcott's *Pantomime* the imaginative-historical Crusoe–Friday relationship – synecdochic of the colonial master–slave one – is reversed when the black man Jackson assumes Crusoe's role:

> For three hundred years I served you … I was your shadow … that was my pantomime … But after a while the child does get frighten of the shadow he make. He say to himself, that is too much obedience, I better hads stop. But the shadow don't stop … until it is the shadow that start dominating the child, it is the servant that start dominating the master …

> (Walcott 1980: 112–13)

Walcott here is gesturing at the decolonizing process, where the 'shadow' begins acquiring mastery, the (black) servant over the (white) master. By deliberately infantilizing the *white* master – infantilizing the colonized native was a standard mode of *colonial* domination – Walcott's black servant is reversing history and racialized cultural relations. Kamau Brathwaite, the Caribbean poet and historian, in his epic *The Arrivants* (1973), while tracing the history of the Middle Passage and the slaving voyages also seeks to connect Caribbean Africans to their African roots. Each of these literary examples serves as an excellent instance of Fanon's argument about the need to free oneself from a legacy so that a new future for the formerly colonized is possible. Fanon, one recalls, argued for a self-reflexive and awakened *consciousness*. It is such a consciousness that we see embodied in these postcolonial texts.

FANON AND POSTCOLONIAL HUMANISM

Fanon's greatest legacy has been his critique of the colonial state as well as his attempts to retrieve a humanism that would be free of the taint of European colonial-capitalist modernity for the postcolonial state. Postcolonial writers (Raja Rao and Mulk Raj Anand in India, Ngũgĩ in Kenya, to name just three) have focused on the necessity for the postcolonial state to simultaneously engage with the colonial past and seek a more emancipatory, democratic and humanist programme directed at the *future*. Both Rao and Ngũgĩ (and we can add Rushdie,

Buchi Emecheta, Soyinka, Walcott and others to the list) are wary, like Fanon, of being mired in the past.

One of the strongest legacies of Fanon has been in postcolonial theory where his emphasis on moving beyond racial and national binaries has appealed to many thinkers. This emphasis on a more universal and inclusive humanism (which we examined in the last chapter) that transcends racial, ethnic and national boundaries has found an interesting heir in postcolonial theorists like Paul Gilroy and Dipesh Chakrabarty.

An interesting appropriation and extension of Fanon may be seen in Dipesh Chakrabarty's project of 'provincializing Europe' (2001). Here Chakrabarty signals his – and that of other postcolonial's – inheritance:

> Postcolonial scholarship is committed, almost by definition, to engaging the universals – such as the abstract figure of the human or that of Reason – that were forged in eighteenth-century Europe and that underlie the human sciences ... Fanon's struggle to hold on to the Enlightenment idea of the human – even when he knew that European imperialism had reduced that idea to the figure of the settler-colonial white man – is now itself a part of the global heritage of all post-colonial thinkers. The struggle ensues because there is no easy way of dispensing with these universals in the condition of political modernity. Without them there would be no social science that addresses issues of modern social justice.
>
> (Chakrabarty 2001: 5)

Chakrabarty thus accepts the Fanonian 'struggle' with European Enlightenment idea(l)s as necessary and inevitable, but this does not, in Chakrabarty's work, as in the case of Fanon, prevent the quest for alternatives.

Chakrabarty's critique of secularist humanism suggests an alternate configuration of the very idea of the political. The old model had no place for gods or superstitions, religious belief or spirits, and thus defined various kinds of non-European thought as 'non-political' because it was irrational and 'poetic'. Despite this, new forms of global cultures that were 'poetic' were visible even during the colonial period. The 'sphere of the political', writes Chakrabarty, does not have to be entirely devoid of 'the agency of gods, spirits, and other super-natural beings' (2001: 12–13). Thus, while on the one hand we see the continuity of particular forms of secular humanism, we also need to see a more inclusive definition of each of these categories: the human, the secular and the political.

In a later work Paul Gilroy has suggested the need for an essence of 'human-ness' minus the (racial) categories within humanity (2000). This 'strategic universalism', as Gilroy terms it, is directed at eliminating categories of race, class and sex, preferring instead a universalism of human dignity. Gilroy here seeks, I think, at once the concreteness of individuals (which would involve markers such as race, gender, class) as well as the abstractions of 'the human'. Fanon had assumed that, as I have argued in the preceding chapter, after the anti-colonial struggle the post-colonial would be more self-reflexive and sensitive. This heightened sensitivity is the ability to respond to both the concrete and the abstract.

Like Fanon, Gilroy recommends moving beyond the traumas of the past to 'self-consciously become more future-oriented' (2000: 335) in a 'planetary humanism' (as he titles one of his chapters). While Gilroy does not spell out these forms of universalism, he comes close, I believe, to what Fanon was trying to theorize and which Ashis Nandy, as I have argued above, articulates as well. Indeed, Gilroy cites *Black Skin*'s closing moments to make his point, proposing that Fanon recognized the horrific nature of both colonial white supremacy and its 'black nationalist shadows' (336). Gilroy accepts that his vision, like Fanon's, is cast in a 'utopian spirit' (336).

As for the postcolonial, formerly colonized's responsibility in developing a self-reflexive, sensitive and more inclusive humanism, we turn once again to Gilroy. Gilroy eloquently argues that Fanon's humanism was the product of a deep engagement with the violence of the colonial condition. Comparing Fanon to Jean Améry, the Auschwitz survivor who had read Fanon, Gilroy writes:

> The humanism these thinkers found and defended came … from profane acts in which the cruelty done by one to another disclosed the urgent obligation to seek an alternative way of being in the world.
>
> (2010: 25)

It is the lived experience of colonialism and its violence (Amery was tortured), Gilroy argues, that causes the colonized to turn humanist. This humanism begins, says Gilroy, with the articulation and acknowledgement of 'racism's debasement of humanity' (2010: 26). That is, only when we acknowledge that racism, especially in colonialism, Nazism and apartheid, has debased the very idea of the human, can we evolve a new humanism.

FURTHER READING

WORKS BY FRANTZ FANON

A Dying Colonialism ([1965] 1970) (trans. Haakon Chevalier), Harmondsworth: Penguin. (Abbreviated as *Dying*)

Black Skin, White Masks ([1956] 2008) (trans. Charles Lam Markmann), London: Pluto (reprint of the 1986 edition). (Abbreviated as *Black Skin*)

The Wretched of the Earth (2004) (trans. Richard Philcox), New York: Grove Press. (Abbreviated as *Wretched*)

Toward the African Revolution (1967) (trans. Haakon Chevalier), New York: Grove. (Abbreviated as *African*)

OTHER RESOURCES OF INTEREST

Gibson, Nigel (ed.) (1999) *Rethinking Fanon: The Continuing Dialogue*, New York: Humanity Press.

A significant volume mainly for the domains in which it locates Fanon – cultural criticism, gender and humanist thought. It includes some of the early commentaries such as Tony Martin's essays on Fanon's psychiatric theories, and works by the first generation of postcolonial scholars (Said, Bhabha, Spivak, Parry). It is also an important volume for its section on Fanon and gender, with essays by Anne McClintock, Diana Fuss and Sharpley-Whiting, among others.

———(2003) *Fanon: The Postcolonial Imagination*, London: Polity.

One of the most exhaustive studies of Fanon, Gibson's work is particularly useful for his examination of the nationalism question in Fanon. Along with Lewis Gordon's work, Gibson's book offers a meticulous examination of Fanon's oeuvre. Gibson's analysis of Fanon's nationalism, violence and humanism are the strengths of the book, even as Gibson takes great care to contextualize Fanon beside Senghor, Sartre and European psychoanalysis. An excellent introduction, if densely written.

Gordon, L. R. (1995) *Fanon and the Crisis of the European Man: An Essay on Philosophy and the Human Sciences*, New York: Routledge.

Gordon's study positions Fanon primarily in relation to the European tradition of humanism. Arguing that Fanon develops his humanist thought only through his engagement with European existential phenomenology, Gordon presents what he terms a philosophical anthropology of Fanon. Not intended as an introduction, but an indispensable account of Fanon nevertheless.

Alessandrini, A. C. (ed.) (1999) *Frantz Fanon: Critical Perspectives*, London and New York: Routledge.

An eclectic collection of essays that suggests the various appropriations and relevance of Fanon for disciplines such as cultural studies, the volume deter-minedly pursues Fanonian legacies. Essays on topics such as Fanon's spectrality (Kawash), the question of representation (Lazarus), cinema and trauma (Kaplan), homosexuality (Goldie) and Fanonian cultural studies (San Juan, Gibson) make this a more wide-ranging volume than an intensive one.

Macey, David (2000) *Frantz Fanon: A Biography*, New York: Picador.

An authoritative account of Fanon's life, Macey's book is meticulously researched, and offers a detailed chronicle of Fanon's otherwise neglected psychiatric writings and life as a medical man. Macey makes extensive use of thus-far untranslated French sources.

Sharpley-Whiting, T. D. (1998) *Frantz Fanon: Conflicts and Feminisms*, Lanham: Rowman and Littlefield.

One of the most sustained examinations of Fanon's gender politics, Sharpley-Whiting's book treats Fanon as a pro-feminist thinker. It refutes, with considerable skill, the accusation that Fanon was sexist, and demonstrates how Fanon's analysis of the Algerian woman revolutionary carries within it the potential revitalization of the woman's role even in postcolonial contexts.

ESSAYS

Alvares, C. (2006) *Humanism and Colonialism*, Oxford: Peter Lang.

Bergner, G. (1999) 'Politics and Pathologies: On the Subject of Race in Psychoanalysis', in A. C. Alessandrini (ed.) *Frantz Fanon: Critical Perspectives*, London and New York: Routledge.

Bernasconi, R. (2001) 'Eliminating the Cycle of Violence: The Place of *A Dying Colonialism* within Fanon's Revolutionary Thought', *Philosophia Africana*, 4 (2): 17–25.

Dane, R. (1994) 'When Mirror Turns Lamp: Frantz Fanon as Cultural Visionary', *Africa Today*, 41 (2): 70–91.

Decker, J. L. (1990–91) 'Terrorism (Un)Veiled: Frantz Fanon and the Women of Algiers', *Cultural Critique*, 17: 177–95.

Fontenot Jr., C. J. (1978) 'Fanon and the Devourers', *Journal of Black Studies*, 9 (1): 93–114.

Gibson, N. (1999a) 'Beyond Manicheanism: Dialectics in the Thought of Frantz Fanon', *Journal of Political Ideologies*, 4 (3): 337–64.

—— (1999b) 'Fanon and the Pitfalls of Cultural Studies', in A. C. Alessandrini (ed.) *Frantz Fanon: Critical Perspectives*, London and New York: Routledge.

—— (2008) 'Upright and Free: Fanon in South Africa, from Biko to the Shackdwellers' Movement (Abahlali base Mjondolo)', *Social Identities*, 14 (6): 683–715.

Gopal, P. (2002) 'Frantz Fanon, Feminism and the Question of Relativism', New Formations, 47: 38–43.

—— (2004) 'Reading Subaltern History', in N. Lazarus (ed.) *The Cambridge Companion to Postcolonial Literary Studies*, Cambridge: Cambridge University Press.

Grohs, G. K. (1968) 'Frantz Fanon and the African Revolution', *Journal of Modern African Studies*, 6 (4): 543–56.

Hansen, E. (1977) *Frantz Fanon: Social and Political Thought*, Columbus: Ohio State University Press.

Hardt, M. and Negri, A. (2000) *Empire*, Cambridge, MA: Harvard University Press.

Ismail, Q. (1992) ' "Boys will be Boys": Gender and National Agency in Fanon and LTTE', *Economic and Political Weekly*, 27 (31–2): 1677–79.

Jeyifo, B. (2007) 'An African Cultural Modernity: Achebe, Fanon, Cabral, and the Philosophy of Decolonization', *Socialism and Democracy*, 21 (3): 125–41.

Jinadu, L. A. (1978) 'Some African Theorists of Culture and Modernization: Fanon, Cabral and Some Others', *African Studies Review*, 21 (1): 121–38.

Macey, D. (2010) ' "I Am My Own Foundation": Frantz Fanon as a Continued Source of Political Embarrassment', *Theory, Culture & Society*, 27 (7–8): 33–51.

Mazrui, A. (1993) 'Language and the Quest for Liberation in Africa: The Legacy of Frantz Fanon', *Third World Quarterly*, 14 (2): 351–63.

Perkins, M. (2005) 'The Role of Colour and "Ethnic" Autobiography: Fanon, Capécia and Difference', *Auto/Biography*, 13: 1–15.

San Juan, Jr., E. (1999) 'Fanon: An Intervention into Cultural Studies', in A. C. Alessandrini (ed.) *Frantz Fanon: Critical Perspectives*, London and New York: Routledge.

Turner, L. (2001) 'Marginal Note on Minority Questions in the Thought of Frantz Fanon', *Philosophia Africana*, 4 (2): 37–46.

—— (2002) '(e)Racing the Ego: Sartre, Modernity, and Fanon's Theory of Consciousness', *Parallax*, 8 (2): 46–53.

Vergès, F. (1997) 'Creole Skin, White Mask: Fanon and Disavowal', *Critical Inquiry*, 23: 578–95.

WORKS CITED

Achebe, C. ([1964] 1977) *Arrow of God*, London: Heinemann.

―― (1988) *Anthills of the Savannah*, London: Heinemann.

Adam, H. M. (1993) 'Frantz Fanon as a Democratic Theorist', *African Affairs*, 92 (369): 499–518.

Ahluwalia, P. (2003) 'Fanon's Nausea: the Hegemony of the White Nation', *Social Identities*, 9 (3): 341–56.

Ahluwalia, P. and Zegeye, A. (2001) 'Frantz Fanon and Steve Biko: Towards Liberation', *Social Identities*, 7 (3): 455–69.

Aidoo, A. A. (1970) *Anowa*, in H. Gilbert (ed.) (2001) *Postcolonial Plays*, London and New York: Routledge.

―― (1977) *Our Sister Killjoy*, Harlow: Longman.

Alessandrini, A. C. ([1998] 2005) 'Humanism in Question: Fanon and Said', in H. Schwarz and S. Ray (eds) *A Companion to Postcolonial Studies*, Cambridge, MA: Blackwell.

―― (2010) 'Small Places, Then and Now: Frantz Fanon, Jamaica Kincaid, and the Futures of Postcolonial Criticism', *Journal of Postcolonial Writing*, 46 (5): 553–64.

Alexander, J. C. (2004) 'Towards a Theory of Cultural Trauma', in J. C. Alexander, R.N. Eyerman, B. Giesen, N. J. Smelser and P. Sztompka (eds) *Cultural Trauma and Collective Identity*, Berkeley: University of California Press.

Appiah, K. A. ([1991] 1997) 'Is the Post- in Postmodernism the Post in Postcolonial?' in P. Mongia (ed.) *Contemporary Postcolonial Theory: A Reader*, New Delhi: Oxford University Press.

Arendt, H. (1970) *On Violence*, New York: Harcourt, Brace, & World, Inc.

Armah, A. K. (1988) *The Beautyful Ones are Not Yet Born*, Portsmouth: Heinemann.

Armstrong, J. ([1993] 1996) 'This is a Story', in J. Thieme (ed.) *The Arnold Anthology of Post-colonial Literatures in English*, London: Arnold.

Azar, M. (1999) 'In the Name of Algeria: Frantz Fanon and the Algerian Revolution', in A. C. Alessandrini (ed.) *Frantz Fanon: Critical Perspectives*, London and New York: Routledge.

Bamyeh, M. A. (2010) 'On Humanizing Abstractions: The Path Beyond Fanon', *Theory, Culture & Society*, 27 (7–8): 52–65.

Baucom, I. (2001) 'Frantz Fanon's Radio: Solidarity, Diaspora, and the Tactics of Listening', *Contemporary Literature*, 42 (1): 15–49.

Bergner, G. (1995) 'Who Is That Masked Woman? Or, the Role of Gender in Fanon's *Black Skin, White Masks*', *PMLA,* 110 (1): 75–88.

Bernasconi, R. (1996) 'Casting the Slough: Fanon's New Humanism for a New Humanity', in L. R. Gordon, T. D. Sharpley-Whiting and R. T. White (eds) *Fanon: A Critical Reader*, London: Blackwell.

—— (2002) 'The Assumption of Negritude: Aimé Césaire, Frantz Fanon, and the Vicious Circle of Racial Politics', *Parallax*, 8 (2): 69–83.

Bhabha, H. K. (2004) 'Framing Fanon'. Foreword in Fanon, *The Wretched of the Earth* (trans. Richard Philcox), New York: Grove.

—— (2008) 'Remembering Fanon: Self, Psyche and the Colonial Condition', Foreword to the 1986 ed. of Fanon, *Black Skin, White Masks* (trans. Charles Lam Markmann), London: Pluto.

—— (2009a) 'Interrogating Identity: Frantz Fanon and the Postcolonial Prerogative', in H. K. Bhabha (1994) *The Location of Culture*, New Delhi: Routledge.

—— (2009b) 'Of Mimicry and Man: The Ambivalence of Colonial Discourse', in H. K. Bhabha (1994) *The Location of Culture*, New Delhi: Routledge.

Boehmer, E. ([1995] 2006) *Colonial and Postcolonial Literature: Migrant Metaphors*, New Delhi: Oxford University Press.

Brathwaite, K. ([1973] 1981) *The Arrivants: A New World Trilogy*, London: Oxford University Press.

Brownmiller, S. (1975) *Against Our Will: Men, Women, and Rape*, New York: Bantam.

Buck, C. (2004) 'Sartre, Fanon, and the Case for Slavery Reparations', *Sartre Studies International*, 10 (2): 123–37.

Bulhan, H. A. (1985) *Frantz Fanon and the Psychology of Oppression*. New York: Plenum Press.

Bullard, A. (2005) 'The Critical Impact of Frantz Fanon and Henri Collomb: Race, Gender, and Personality Testing of North and West Africans', *Journal of the History of the Behavioral Sciences*, 41 (3): 225–48.

Butts, H. F. (1979) 'Frantz Fanon's Contributions to Psychiatry: The Psychology of Racism and Colonialism', *Journal of the National Medical Association*, 71 (10): 1015–18.

Caute, D. ([1969] 1970) *Fanon*, New York: Viking.

Césaire, A. (1972) *Discourse on Colonialism* (trans. Joan Pinkham), New York and London: Monthly Review Press.

Chakrabarty, D. (2001) *Provincializing Europe: Postcolonial Thought and Historical Difference*, Oxford University Press.

Chow, R. (1999) 'The Politics of Admittance: Female Sexual Agency, Miscegenation, and the Formation of Community in Frantz Fanon', in A. C. Alessandrini (ed.) *Frantz Fanon: Critical Perspectives*, London and New York: Routledge.

Christian, L. (2005) 'Fanon and the Trauma of the Cultural Message', *Textual Practice*, 19 (3): 219–41.

Cornell, D. (2001) 'The Secret Behind the Veil: A Reinterpretation of "Algeria Unveiled"', *Philosophia Africana*, 4 (2): 27–35.

Crane, R. J. (2001) 'Out of the Center: Thoughts on the Post-colonial Literatures of Australia and New Zealand', in Gregory Castle (ed.) *Postcolonial Discourses: An Anthology*, Oxford: Blackwell.

Dangarembga, T. (1988) *Nervous Conditions*, London: The Women's Press.

Djebar, A. (1999) *Women of Algiers in their Apartment* (trans. M. de Jager), Charlottesville and London: University Press of Virginia.

Doane, M. A. (1991) *Femmes Fatales: Feminism, Film Theory, Psychoanalysis*, New York: Routledge.

Dollimore, J. (1991) *Sexual Dissidence: Augustine to Wilde, Freud to Foucault*, Oxford: Oxford University Press.

Dubey, M. (1998) 'The "True Lie" of the Nation: Fanon and Feminism', *Differences,* 10 (2): 1–29.

DuBois, W. E. B. (1961) *The Souls of Black Folk: Essays and Sketches*, Forgotten Books. Available at http://www.forgottenbooks.org/info/The_Souls_of_Black_Folk_1000095666.php

Eaglestone, R. ([2004] 2009) *The Holocaust and the Postmodern*, Oxford: Oxford University Press.

El Saadawi, N. (1980) *The Hidden Face of Eve: Women in the Arab World* (trans. and ed., S. Hetata), London: Zed Books.

Farah, N. (1999) *Maps*, New York: Arcade.

Faulkner, R. A. (1996) 'Assia Djebar, Frantz Fanon, Women, Veils, and Land', *World Literature Today*, 96 (70): 847–55.

Feuchtwang, S. (1987) 'Fanonian Spaces', *New Formations*, 1: 124–30.

Forsdick, C. and Murphy, D. (2009) 'The Rise of the Francophone Postcolonial Intellectual: The Emergence of a Tradition', *Modern and Contemporary France*, 17 (2): 163–75.

Fuss, D. (1994) 'Interior Colonies: Frantz Fanon and the Politics of Identification', *Diacritics*, 24 (2–3): 20–42.

Gandhi, L. (1999) *Postcolonial Theory: A Critical Introduction*, New Delhi: Oxford University Press.

—— (2006) *Affective Communities: Anticolonial Thought and the Politics of Friendship*, New Delhi: Permanent Black.

Gates Jr., H. L. (1991) 'Critical Fanonism', *Critical Inquiry*, 17 (3): 457–70.

Gauch, S. (2002) 'Fanon on the Surface', *Parallax*, 8 (2): 116–28.

Geismer, D. (1971) *Fanon*, New York: Dial.

Gendzier, I. ([1973] 1985) *Frantz Fanon: A Critical Study*, New York: Grove Press.

Gibson, N. (2003) *Fanon: The Postcolonial Imagination*, London: Polity.

Gilroy, P. (2000) *Against Race: Imagining Political Culture Beyond the Color Line*, Massachusetts: Harvard University Press.

—— (2010) 'Fanon and Améry: Theory, Torture and the Prospect of Humanism', *Theory, Culture & Society*, 27 (7–8): 16–32.

Goldie, T. (1999) 'Saint Fanon and Homosexual Territory', in A. C. Alessandrini (ed.) *Frantz Fanon: Critical Perspectives*, London and New York: Routledge.

Gordon, L. R. (1995) *Fanon and the Crisis of the European Man: An Essay on Philosophy and the Human Sciences*, New York: Routledge.

—— (2006) 'Through the Zone of Nonbeing: A Reading of *Black Skin, White Masks* in Celebration of Fanon's Eightieth Birthday', *Worlds and Knowledges Otherwise*, available online at http://www.jhfc.duke.edu/wko/dossiers/1.3/LGordon.pdf (accessed 9 December 2010).

Haddour, A. (2005) 'Sartre and Fanon: On Negritude and Political Participation', *Sartre Studies International*, 11 (1–2): 286–301.

—— (2010) 'Torture Unveiled: Reading Fanon and Bourdieu in the Context of May 1958', *Theory, Culture & Society*, 27 (7–8): 66–90.

Hage, G. (2010) 'The Affective Politics of Racial Mis-interpellation', *Theory, Culture & Society*, 27 (7–8): 112–29.

Hall, S. (1996) 'Why Fanon, Why Now, Why *Black Skin, White Masks?*', in A. Read (ed.) *The Fact of Blackness: Frantz Fanon and Visual Representation*, Seattle: Bay Press.

Hanley, D. (1976) 'Frantz Fanon: Revolutionary Nationalist', *Political Studies*, 24 (2): 120–31.

Hatem, M. (1993) 'Toward the Development of Post-Islamist and Post-Nationalist Feminist Discourses in the Middle East', in J. Tucker (ed.) *Arab Women: Old Boundaries, New Frontiers*, Bloomington: Indiana University Press.

Helie-Lucas, M. (1990) 'Women, Nationalism, and Religion in Algerian National Liberation Struggle', in M. Badran and M. Cooke (eds) *Opening the Gates: A Century of Arab Feminist Writing*, Bloomington: Indiana University Press.

Hook, D. (2005) 'A Critical Psychology of the Postcolonial', *Theory and Psychology*, 15 (4): 375–403.

hooks, b. (1996) 'Feminism as a Persistent Critique: What's Love Got to Do With It?', in Alan Read (ed.) *The Fact of Blackness: Frantz Fanon and Visual Representation*, Seattle: Bay Press.

Hosain, A. ([1961] 1988) *Sunlight on a Broken Column*, New York: Penguin-Virago.

Ignatieff, M. (2001) *Human Rights as Politics and Idolatry*, (ed.) Amy Guttman, Princeton: Princeton University Press.

Innes, C. L. (2007) *The Cambridge Introduction to Postcolonial Literatures in English*, Cambridge: Cambridge University Press.

James, J. (1997) *Transcending the Talented Tenth: Black Leaders and American Intellectuals*, New York: Routledge.

JanMohamed, A. (1985) 'The Economy of Manichean Allegory: The Function of Racial Difference in Colonialist Literature', *Critical Inquiry*, 12 (1): 59–87.

Jean-Marie, V. (2007) *Fanon: Collective Ethics and Humanism*, New York: Peter Lang.

Kawash, S. (1999) 'Terrorists and Vampires: Fanon's Spectral Violence of Decolonization', in A. C. Alessandrini (ed.) *Frantz Fanon: Critical Perspectives*, London and New York: Routledge.

Keller, R. C. (2007) 'Clinician and Revolutionary: Frantz Fanon, Biography, and the History of Colonial Medicine', *Bulletin of the History of Medicine,* 81 (4) (2007): 823–841.

Keneally, T. (1973) *The Chant of Jimmie Blacksmith*, Victoria: Penguin.

Kincaid, J. (1988) *A Small Place*, New York: Farrar, Straus and Giroux.

Krautwurst, U. (2003) 'What is Settler Colonialism? An Anthropological Meditation on Frantz Fanon's "Concerning Violence"', *History and Anthropology*, 14 (1): 55–72.

Lazarus, N. (1993) 'Disavowing Decolonization: Fanon, Nationalism, and the Problematic of Representation in Current Theories of Colonial Discourse', *Research in African Literatures*, 24 (4): 69–98.

—— (1994) 'National Consciousness and the Specificity of (Post)colonial Intellectualism', in F. Barker, P. Hulme and M. Iversen (eds) *Colonial Discourse/Postcolonial Theory*, Manchester: Manchester University Press.

Lebeau, V. (1998) 'Psychopolitics: Fanon's *Black Skin, White Masks*', in J. Campbell and L. Harbord (eds) *Psycho-politics and Cultural Desires*, London: UCL Press.

Macey, D. (1999) 'The Recall of the Real: Frantz Fanon and Psychoanalysis', *Constellations*, 6 (1): 97–107.

—— (2000) *Frantz Fanon: A Biography*, New York: Picador.

—— (2004) 'Frantz Fanon, or the Difficulty of Being Martinican', *History Workshop Journal*, 58: 212–23.

Mama, A. (1995) *Beyond the Masks: Race, Gender, Subjectivity*, New York: Routledge.

Mannoni, O. (1950 [1964]) *Prospero and Caliban: The Psychology of Colonization* (trans. Pamela Powesland), London: Methuen.

Mardorossian, C. (2009) 'From Fanon to Glissant: A Martinican Genealogy', *Small Axe*, 30: 12–24.

Martin, T. (1970) 'Rescuing Fanon from the Critics', *African Studies Review*, 13 (3): 381–99.

Martinez, J. M. (2003) 'On the Possibility of the Latino Postcolonial Intellectual', *Nepantla*, 4 (2): 253–6.

McClintock, A. (1995) *Imperial Leather: Race, Gender and Sexuality in the Colonial Context*, London and New York: Routledge.

—— (1999) 'Fanon and Gender Agency', in N. Gibson (ed.) *Rethinking Fanon*, London and New York: Routledge.

McCulloch, J. (1983) *Black Soul, White Artifact: Fanon's Clinical Psychology and Social Theory*, Cambridge: Cambridge University Press.

Memmi, A. (1973) 'The Impossible Life of Frantz Fanon', *The Massachusetts Review*, 14 (1): 9–39.

Mercer, K. (1999) 'Busy in the Ruins of a Wretched Phantasia', in A. C. Alessandrini (ed.) *Frantz Fanon: Critical Perspectives*, London and New York: Routledge.

Mernissi, F. (1987) *Beyond the Veil: Male-Female Dynamics in Modern Muslim Society*, Bloomington: Indiana University Press.

Mignolo, W. D. (2005) 'Human Understanding and (Latin) American Interests – The Politics and Sensibilities of Geohistorical Locations', in H. Schwarz and S. Ray (eds) *A Companion to Postcolonial Studies*, Cambridge, MA: Blackwell.

Mistry, R. ([1995] 1996) *A Fine Balance*, London: Faber and Faber.

Moore, T. O. (2005) 'A Fanonian Perspective on Double Consciousness', *Journal of Black Studies*, 35 (6): 751–62.

Moraga, C. (2001) *The Hungry Woman* [including *The Hungry Woman: A Mexican Medea* and *Heart of the Earth: A Popul Vuh Story*], Albuquerque: West End Press.

Mowitt, J. (1992) 'Algerian Nation: Fanon's Fetish', *Cultural Critique*, 22: 165–86.

Mudimbe, V. Y. (1988) *The Invention of Africa: Gnosis, Philosophy, and the Order of Knowledge*, Bloomington and Indianapolis: Indiana University Press.

Naipaul, V. S. ([1962] 1969) *The Middle Passage*, Harmondsworth: Penguin.

—— (1987) *The Enigma of Arrival*, London: Viking.

Nandy, A. (1987) 'Towards a Third World Utopia', in A. Nandy (2004) *Bonfire of Creeds: The Essential Ashis Nandy*, Delhi: Oxford University Press.

—— (1992) *Traditions, Tyranny, and Utopias: Essays in the Politics of Awareness*, Delhi: Oxford University Press.

—— (1998) 'A New Cosmopolitanism: Toward a Dialogue of Asian Civilizations', in Kuan-Hsing Chen (ed.), *Trajectories: Inter-Asia Cultural Studies*, London and New York: Routledge, pp. 142–9.

Nayar, P. K. (2008a) *Postcolonial Literature: An Introduction*, New Delhi: Pearson-Longman.

—— (2008b) 'Affective Cosmopolitanism: Ashis Nandy's Utopia', available online at http://www.esocialsciences.com/articles/displayArticles.asp?Article_ID=1732

—— (2010) *Postcolonialism: A Guide for the Perplexed*, London and New York: Continuum.

Ngwarsungu, C. (1990) 'The Rhythms of Literary Ideas: Characterization in African Literature', *Journal of Black Studies,* 20 (4): 467–86.

Omar, S. M. (2009) 'Fanon in Algeria: A Case of Horizontal (Post)-colonial Encounter?', *Journal of Transatlantic Studies*, 7 (3): 264–78.

Parry, B. (1987) 'Problems in Current Theories of Colonial Discourse', *Oxford Literary Review,* 9 (1–2): 27–58.

—— (1994) 'Resistance Theory/Theorizing Resistance or Two Cheers for Nativism', in F. Barker, P. Hulme and M. Iversen (eds) *Colonial Discourse/ Postcolonial Theory*, Manchester: Manchester University Press.

Paxton, N. L. (1999) *Writing Under the Raj: Gender, Race, and Rape in the British Colonial Imagination, 1830–1947*, Brunswick: Rutgers University Press.

Pithouse, R. (2003) '"That the Tool Never Possess the Man": Taking Fanon's Humanism Seriously', *Politikon*, 30 (2): 107–31.

Posnock, R. (1997) 'How It Feels to Be a Problem: Du Bois, Fanon, and the "Impossible Life" of the Black Intellectual', *Critical Inquiry*, 23 (2): 323–49.

Prabhu, A. (2006) 'Narration in Frantz Fanon's *Peau noire masques blancs*: Some Reconsiderations', *Research in African Literatures*, 37 (4): 189–210.

Rabaka, R. (2009) *Africana Critical Theory: Reconstructing the Black Radical Tradition, from W. E. B. Du Bois and C. L. R. James to Frantz Fanon and Amilcar Cabral*, New York: Lexington.

Rajan, R. S. (1997) 'The Third World Academic in Other Places; or, The Postcolonial Intellectual Revisited', *Critical Inquiry*, 23: 596–616.

Rao, R. ([1938] 1963) *Kanthapura*, New York: New Directions.

Read, A. (ed.) (1996) *Facts of Blackness: Frantz Fanon and Visual Representation*, Seattle: Bay Press.

Roberts, N. (2004) 'Fanon, Sartre, Violence, and Freedom', *Sartre Studies International*, 10 (2): 139–60.

Rushdie, S. (1981) *Midnight's Children*, London: Jonathan Cape.

Scott, J. C. (1985) *Weapons of the Weak: Everyday Forms of Peasant Resistance*, New Haven and London: Yale University Press.

Sekyi-Otu, A. (1996) *Fanon's Dialectic of Experience*, Cambridge, MA: Harvard University Press.

Serequeberhan, T. (1994) *The Hermeneutics of African Philosophy: Horizon and Discourse*, New York: Routledge.

Seshadri-Crooks, K. (2002) '"I am a Master": Terrorism, Masculinity, and Political Violence in Frantz Fanon', *Parallax*, 8 (2): 84–98.

Sharpe, J. (1993) *Allegories of Empire: The Figure of Woman in the Colonial Text*, Minneapolis and London: University of Minnesota Press.

Sharpley-Whiting, T. D. (1998) *Frantz Fanon: Conflicts and Feminisms*, Lanham: Rowman and Littlefield.

Shome, R. (2006) 'Thinking Through the Diaspora: Call Centers, India, and a New Politics of Hybridity', *International Journal of Cultural Studies*, 9 (1): 105–24.

Slaughter, J. R. (2007) *Human Rights, Inc.: The World Novel, Narrative Form and International Law*, New York: Fordham University Press.

Slisli, F. (2008) 'Islam: The Elephant in Fanon's *The Wretched of the Earth*', *Critique: Critical Middle Eastern Studies*, 17 (1): 97–108.

Soyinka, W. (1964) 'Telephone Conversation', in J. Reed and C. Wake, *A Book of African Verse*, London: Heinemann, pp. 80–2.

—— (1975) *Death and the King's Horseman*, in W. Soyinka (1984) *Six Plays*, London: Methuen.

—— (1996) *The Open Sore of a Continent: A Personal Narrative of the Nigerian Crisis*, New York: Oxford University Press.

Srivastava, N. (2010) 'Towards a Critique of Colonial Violence: Fanon, Gandhi and the Restoration of Agency', *Journal of Postcolonial Writing*, 46 (3): 303–19.

Taylor, C. (1994) 'The Politics of Recognition', in L. T. Goldberg (ed.) *Multiculturalism: A Critical Reader*, Cambridge: Blackwell.

Tucker, G. E. (1978) 'Machiavelli and Fanon: Ethics, Violence and Action', *Journal of Modern African Studies*, 16 (3): 397–415.

Vaughan, M. (1993) 'Madness and Colonialism, Colonialism as Madness: Re-Reading Fanon, Colonialism Discourse and the Psychopathology of Colonialism', *Paideuma*, 39: 45–55.

Vergès, F. (1996) 'Chains of Madness, Chains of Colonialism: Fanon and Freedom', in A. Read (ed.) *The Fact of Blackness: Frantz Fanon and Visual Representation*, Seattle: Bay Press.

—— (2010) ' "There are No Blacks in France": Fanonian Discourse, the "Dark Night of Slavery" and the French Civilizing Mission Reconsidered', *Theory, Culture & Society,* 27 (7–8): 91–111.

Vivaldi, J-M. (2007) *Fanon: Collective Ethics and Humanism*, New York: Peter Lang.

Walcott, D. (1970) *Dream on Monkey Mountain and Other Plays*, New York: Farrar, Straus and Giroux.

—— (1980) *Remembrance & Pantomime*, New York: Farrar, Straus and Giroux.

Walder, D. (1998) *Post-colonial Literatures in English: History, Language, Theory*, Oxford: Blackwell.

Wallach Scott, J. (2007) *The Politics of the Veil*, Princeton, NJ: Princeton University Press.

Wallerstein, I. (1979) *The Capitalist World-Economy*, Cambridge: Cambridge University Press.

Wa Thiong'O, Ngũgĩ (1965) *The River Between*, London: Heinemann.

—— (1967) *A Grain of Wheat*, London: Heinemann.

—— (1972) *Homecoming: Essays*, London: Heinemann.

Wilder, G. (2004) 'Race, Reason, Impasse: Césaire, Fanon, and the Legacy of Emancipation', *Radical History Review*, 90: 31–61.

Wilmot, P. (2009) 'The Role of Violence in the Works of Wright and Fanon', *The Black Scholar*, 39 (1–2): 17–22.

Woddis, J. (1972) *New Theories of Revolution: A Commentary on the Views of Frantz Fanon, Régis Debray and Herbert Marcuse*, London: Lawrence and Wishart.

Yeğenoğlu, M. (1998) *Colonial Fantasies: Towards a Feminist Reading of Orientalism*, Cambridge: Cambridge University Press.

Young, R. (1990) *White Mythologies: Writing History and the West*, London: Routledge.

INDEX